Sakshi

Vol. - 60

AYODHYA MAHATMYA

The Glory of Ayodhya

Skanda Purana

Translated by
ANURADHA GOYAL

Vani Book Company
An imprint of Vani Prakashan Group

First Edition : 2021
Second Edition : 2024

Vani Book Company

An imprint of Vani Prakashan Group

4695, 21-A, Daryaganj, New Delhi 110 002
Phone : +91 11 23273167 Fax : +91 11 23275710
India

Branches

Ashok Rajpath, Patna 800 004, Bihar

Coffee House Campus, Mahatma Gandhi Marg, Prayagraj -211 001, Uttar Pradesh

Mahatma Gandhi International Hindi University, Wardha- 442 001, Maharashtra

Motia Park Opp. Water Tank, Sultania Road, Bhopal- 462 001, Madhya Pradesh

Goripur Taliya Para, 313, R.B.C. Road 24- Parganas (North) Kolkata-743 166, West Bengal

sales@vaniprakashan.in
vaniprakashan@gmail.com

In Association with

ESTD.-1986

Ayodhya Research Institute
presents

AYODHYA MAHATMYA : THE GLORY OF AYODHYA
SKANDA PURANA
Translated by Anuradha Goyal

ISBN : 978-93-90678-17-4
Religion/Culture

Price : ₹ 299

Printed at City Press, Delhi-110 095 (India)

Vani Prakashan's signature motif is created by Artist Maqbool Fida Husain

Dedicated to

All Ayodhyawasis – past, present & future

Introduction

Ayodhya is the Adipuri of Vishnu, his first city. It is the first among *Saptapuri*[1] - the seven *Mokshadayini*[2] or salvation giving cities around India. It is the base for one of the two epics, the two *Itihasa* from India - Ramayana. Poets like Valmiki, Tulsidas, Kalidas have written glorious accounts of Ayodhya, as have poets and storytellers in every other language in India. Translations of literary works and performances of various art forms have taken Ayodhya to the world wrapped in the story of Ramayana.

In the popular memory, it is the place where the seventh avatar of Vishnu, Sri Ramtook birth in *Treta Yug*. This is the city that he returned to rule from after his fourteen years of exile that took him across the country and even across the ocean to Lanka. Ayodhya though has seen many more stories unfold on its land besides the story of Maryada Purushottam Ram. It has been a witness to a long line of illustrious kings of *Suryavansh* or the solar dynasty who ruled from here. Ayodhya Mahatmya of Skanda Puran captures the place as the land of Suryavanshi kings, as a pilgrimage place for the sages and common devotees across different eras and as a land that puts you on the path of Moksha. It is the *Sthala Purana* of the city of Vishnu, telling us the glory of the city through the stories of its various sacred spots, of the city that is believed to sit on Vishnu's Chakra, rising above the earth.

Skanda Puran is longest of the eighteen mahapuranas with more than 80,000 shlokas in it. It is divided into nine *Khandas*, each of which takes us to a different region and tells us about its scared geography. Ayodhya Mahatmya comes in the Vaishnav Khand of Skanda Puran.In 990 shlokas spread across 10 chapters, it takes us through the stories of each of the Tirtha Sthala or the holy spots in the city. In these stories, it covers the stories of many kings who ruled from Ayodhya, stories of many sages and devatas who performed tapasya here and the merits it brings for the common pilgrims. It talks about the various Yatras that happen around the year at each of these places mentioned in Ayodhya. All the stories put together create a cultural and spiritual history and heritage of Ayodhya, the very reason it is such an important Tirtha.

The narrative of Ayodhya Mahatmya takes us through a series of ponds or Kunds that brings out the inherent relationship of humanity with water. Many of the stories talks about the different ghats of Sarayu. The confluence of Sarayu with Tilodaki and Gharghara[3] rivers are highlighted as the holiest of spots, just like the confluence of any two rivers is revered in India. Despite having three rivers surrounding the city, there are a series of ponds excavated around the city. Many of these can still be seen in the city. What is fascinating is the exact map that is created by the authors of Skanda Puran of these ponds with exact placement of each one, with respect to the others.

The rituals and the merits they bring to the pilgrim have been described for each place. One may find them repeated again and again. I wondered why would they repeat it so many times and then I realised that this was done to emphasize the point, by telling it in as many ways as possible. English is limited by the vocabulary it has for describing sacred rituals of India. So, words and phrases may seem repeating more than they look in the original text, where the repetitions have a nuanced difference.

Each Tirtha when described is described as the ultimate Tirtha, unparalleled by any other Tirtha in the universe. Many Tirthas are described as the ones where rest of the Tirthas come to wash their sins, while others are described lowly in comparison. We have to see in the context of time and space when these scriptures were written. Travel and pilgrimage places were not so easily accessible and people would have needed very strong reasons to travel to these places associated with the avatars of deities. They must go back with the satisfaction that they have visited the ultimate Tirtha and need not visit the other ones. It is also believed that the most important Tirtha is the one you are visiting at the moment. So, in the moment of your visit, every Tirtha is the most important tirtha.

Snan or taking holy bath in the waters is most often mentioned activity at a Tirtha. More often than not it is like taking a dip in the water to wash off all the sins accumulated so far, preparing yourself for a better place in the afterlife. Every Tirtha mentioned has a waterbody associated with it, be it a river, a pond or a well. The most important of these is the confluence of two rivers, at the place where they merge and become one.

Dana or donations are always associated with a pilgrimage. There is a Dakshina that you pay to a purohit for his services in helping you perform the rituals. However, the virtue is associated with dana or the donation that you do at the Tirtha. There are different types of dana mentioned throughout the

Mahatmya like food, clothes, ornaments, cows and gold. It was a pleasant surprise to see that nowhere money is mentioned to be donated, unless you count gold as global currency of the olden times.

Since Dana is mentioned as essential part of every pilgrimage and every ritual, you also gather what constitutes a Dana. Like everything is India, there is no standard quantity that is prescribed for everyone. It is repeatedly mentioned that one should give Dana *Yathashaktior* as per one's capacity to give. It is not mentioned explicitly but the focus on this word indicates that one should not go beyond one's means to donate in the hope of a better afterlife or earning good karma. One should donate for sure, definitely at a Tirtha, but not beyond one's capacity to give. At the same time, it also says you should not be miserly when donating.

It is probably repeated often to discourage any influence from wealthy pilgrims who may be donating a lot more or giving in to greedy people who may try to convince you to give everything you have. There are always alternatives mentioned for ones who may not be able to afford big donations like just lighting a lamp.

Who should be given the dana is also emphasised every time the dana is mentioned? It says one should give it to the Brahmins who are truly engaged in pursuing Vedas, those who are of good conduct, stay clean and perform all the rituals including all the *Yama*[4] and *Niyama*[5] prescribed for them. It is equally emphasized that donating to an undeserving candidate harms both the donor and the receiver.

Rituals of Shan and Dana are always mentioned with the word '*Vidhi*[6]'. This essentially means one should do the rituals as per the established norms. No norms are mentioned though anywhere in this text. It is assumed that the local Brahmins are well versed with these rituals and one must take their help to conduct rituals. This may have been done to prevent any deviations as well as to ensure livelihood for local Brahmins. To me, this also defined the limits of a Mahatmya that tells you the glory of a place and does not get into the ritualistic details although all prescribed rituals are mentioned. It may also be assumed that rituals were performed differently for people from different lineages. They would be covered elsewhere in some other texts.

For some specific places, there is mention of *Deep Dana* or lighting a lamp. At a couple of places, it is recommended to do *Jagran* or keeping awake through the night while praying to the deity. At some temples, some *Utsava* or festive celebrations are recommended with music, singing and dancing.

Stutis or poems of glory, are chanted by various people in different stories mentioned in the Mahatmya. Some are sung to invoke Hari, while others are sung upon getting his *darshana* and yet others are sung just for the pure devotion towards the Vishnu. One of the Stuti is even sung by Shankara for Vishnu. All these stutis are poetic in nature and have a rhythm to them that I have tried to maintain in the translation. It is often said in the text that one who sings these Stutis will get similar results like the one who originally sang it.

The Setting

Indian scriptures are always a conversation between two or more people. The setting is explained, the presence of every noteworthy person is mentioned before the dialogues starts. Knowledge is shared only when a question is asked. This essentially means that you the seeker must have a query, an inquisitiveness, a curiosity in your mind, to ask the question. When the seeker is ready, the answer is provided.

The person who answers, usually a learned sage, begins by first acknowledging his source of knowledge. He mentions, when he asked the same or similar question to one of his elders and how it was answered. Sometimes, there is a series of people who have asked the same question, to establish the lineage through which it has come to the person, who is now ready to answer or share it. During the course of main dialogues, sometimes another dialogue comes as part of narration, like a sub-plot in the main plot. Ayodhya Mahatmya is primarily a dialogue between Rishi Agastya and Maharishi Ved Vyasa, though it is being narrated by Suta to almost every saint and sage present at Kurukshetra.

First chapter takes the reader to Kurukshetra, explains the setting in which Ved Vyasa tells the Ayodhya Mahatmya to Suta, along with Rishis who have gathered from all over India. The setting tells us that it was a tradition for different sages and saints from different parts of the country to periodically congregate at Tirtha Sthalas for Yagnas or for ritual baths. This was a place where they exchanged notes. In this particular text, they all exchange their travelogues of visiting different places since they last met. They all request Suta Rishi to tell them the glory of Ayodhya, who obliges them.

He begins by telling them how he heard this from Ved Vyasa, who in turn had heard it from Agastaya Rishi after the later went for a pilgrimage to Ayodhya. There is a physical description of Ayodhya beginning with its dimensions along the Sarayu river. City is described along with its people, flora and fauna. Then begins the story of *Vishnu Hari* that gets its name from a Brahmin Vishnu Sharma who performed tapasya here in the past.

Second Chapter tells us about the important Tirthas of Ayodhya and the story behind them that makes them such important Tirthas. It talks about Brahmakund created by Brahma, Rinmochana Tirtha where one can get rid of all kinds of debts and Paapamochan Tirtha that helps you get rid of the effects of bad deeds one may have done while giving the exact location of each of them with respect to each other and banks of Sarayu.

The biggest Tirtha mentioned in this chapter is Sahastradhara that is connected with the story of Lakshman, the younger brother of Ram and an avatar of Sheshnag. Sahastradhara is an important pilgrimage place on the Sarayu riverfront in Ayodhya and continues to be visited by the pilgrims with devotion.

Third Chapter talks about Swargdwara as one of the most pious places in Ayodhya and on whole of earth by talking about different sages, devatas and even Tirthas who visit Swargdwara.

Chandrahari is one of the seven Vishnu Murtis famous in Ayodhya. Its story is the focal point of this chapter. If you have ever wondered why we Indians do not celebrate special birthdays or anniversaries like silver or golden jubilee, here is the answer. This is a place where people come to celebrate witnessing of a thousand full moons in life or roughly eighty-three years and four months. An elaborate ritual is performed that pays respect to moon in its various forms.

Chapter four takes us from Chandrahari to Dharmahari. The simple story of Dharmahari tells us that just the delight of being in the space of Vishnu can give you his darshana.

Story of gold mine talks about the relationship between the righteous king, learned sages and the public through the story of Raghu. Raghu goes around and wins the world and rules the earth from Ayodhya. However, he gives away everything he earned to the Brahmins after a Yagna, only to find one of them not satisfied. He again steps out to get the dakshina for him and stops only after he is satisfied. In the process, he gets ample gold. Heaga in gives it away to the Brahmins and uses it for protection of his people. It is a powerful story that tells us about the nature of kings, their role in the society that involves taking care of all the needs of the people in his reign.

Chapter five is the smallest chapter of Ayodhya Mahatmya. It continues with the backstory of Swarnkhani Tirtha described in the previous chapter telling us why did Vishmamitra ask for so much of gold. I found this story very intriguing as it tells us about the dharma of various sections of society. It tells us that a king does not earn for himself or to live a luxurious life. He earns to give it away to the learned Brahmins so that they can pursue knowledge and to protect his people. It tells us that a saint who comes to you to ask for something must not return disappointed even if what he asks for is way beyond your capability to give. It tells us that when you wage war for the right reasons, your enemies bow down to you. It tells us that as a saint or a renunciate, you must take what you really need to survive and not let your greed overtake you. It tells us that a Guru's Dakshina must be paid for, even if he does not expect it or he lets you barter it with the service you do for the Guru. It tells us about the respectful relationship between two revered Gurus like Vishwamitra and Durvasa, who may play around with each other but never get offended. It is one of the most beautiful stories in this section of Skanda Puran.

It then goes on to tell us about the confluence of Sarayu and Tilodaki river which is also a Tirtha of the Ayodhya Kshetra.

Chapter six is the longest chapter and rightly so as it describes the glory of Gopratara Tirtha in detail. This is the place associated with the departure of Sri Ram from Ayodhya, and from this earth to merge back with his real form of Vishnu, in the Vaikuntha. The scene of his departure is described in detail with every possible creature on earth and in the heavens being either a part of it or a witness to it.

Chapter Seven and eight focusses on lots of ponds across the city of Ayodhya. Each pond has a story that is told sometimes in detail and sometimes in passing. The merits are always associated with taking a bath in these holy ponds and by giving donations there. Most ponds have a specific date when an annual pilgrimage is recommended there, when the bath there is even more beneficial. For example, tirthas associated with deities like Sun are more beneficial on Sunday, the day ruled by Sun. Each pond is mentioned with respect to earlier pond mentioned like a chain that one can follow. During my travels in Ayodhya, I could trace many of these ponds.

In the end, Vasishtha Muni tells the glory of Ayodhya as a Tirtha. He lists the sequence in which a pilgrim should visit these various Tirthas in the city. The same has been reproduced for easy reference at the end of the book.

Chapter Nine focussed on the Tirthas around Nandigram – the place where Bharat lived outside the city limits of Ayodhya during the 14-year exile of Sri Ram. The place has many ponds associated with the story of Sri Ram's exile. It is the place from where he left for his exile and this is the place where he returned to and gave up his forest avatar before entering the city of Ayodhya. Places mentioned in this chapter include Bharatkund, Gaya Koop and Jatakund.

Chapter Ten concludes the Mahatmya by telling us that a pilgrimage must be done with the purity of mind first. A dip in the holy river is meaningful only if your heart and mind are pure and devoid of any negative emotions. It beautifully sums us the glory of Ayodhya with these wise words. In light of this chapter, when I look back at the text, I see that it helps us pursue all the four Purushart has of human life – Dharma, Artha, Kama & Moksha. Moksha, that is the final goal of human life is obviously given more importance but the other three are not ignored.

As the Mahatmya says, anyone who narrates this and everyone who listen to this or reads this too gets the merits of visiting the city of Vishnu. So, here is praying for Vishnu Kripa on all of us.

Sapta Hari – Ayodhya had seven famous Vishnu Murtis, each with a different pre-fix and with a unique story. All these seven murtis had Vishnu in his four-armed form holding conch, discus and mace in his hands. Padma is not mentioned in the text. Sapta-Hari Murtis include - Guptahari, Chakrahari, Vishnuhari, Chandrahari, Bilvahari, Dharmahari and Punyahari. As of now you can see one of these at a small temple on Guptaar Ghat. Not much is known about the rest of them. Five of these have stories in the Ayodhya Mahatmya of Skanda Puran. Bilvahari and Punyahari are not mentioned in this text, but their stories can be heard in Ayodhya.

Reference

1. Saptapuri refers to seven ancient cities – Ayodhya, Mathura, Maya or Haridwar, Kashi or Varanasi, Kanchi or Kanchipuram, Avantika or Ujjain and Dwaravati or Dwarka
2. Bestower of liberation from the cycle of birth and death
3. Also known as Ghaghra
4. Self Restraints
5. Prescribed observances like daily worships
6. Prescribed set of rituals usually known to the local priests

Sri Vishnu

Translator's Note

As a translator, my focus is to make sure that the essence of the story and the place is conveyed to you. Every language has its own way of conveying things. Plus, language is an integral part of a culture and so is Sanskrit to Indian culture. Thus, at times it is a tough task to find the perfect translation and the translators understanding or interpretation is bound to creep in. I have tried to explain as many Indian terms as possible in the footnotes. They have been explained at the first mention and then the term has been used assuming the reader understands it.

There are elaborate Stutis for each character, be it the sages, saints, deities or even the common priests when they are first introduced. Most of these adjectives are not really translatable. Even when there is a word available in English, it really does not convey the meaning. So, I have pruned some long descriptions at some places, wherever it was possible to do so without losing any meaning.

I have kept the dialogue between Agastya and Ved Vyasa in present tense, and the ones they refer to in their conversation in the past tense. I have used this discretion to keep the reader in the present, as if we are listening to this conversation between the two of them.

Calendar of all the festivals with their dates and prescribed activities has been compiled into a table for the easy use of the reader. At one place the order of pilgrimage is mentioned, the same has been listed in the Annexure. There is one order mentioned in the last chapter as well, but that would be for a long-term pilgrim who can spend a year and attend all festivals on the prescribed dates. If you plan to do that, then just follow the calendar mentioned at the end of the book.

We have also created a map of all the Tirthas as mentioned in the text. A list of these directions is appended in the annexure for ready reference

CONTENTS

Chapter 1

City of Ayodhya & Chakra Tirtha

The setting for this dialogue is in Kurukshetra[1]. Here the sages from all over have gathered for the 12-year long yagnas performed by the noble king Ram[2]. Munis from Himalayas, who are experts in Vedas, the knowers of three times[3] (past, present and future) from Naimisharanya, those who live in the forests of Dandakaranya, Arbudaranya, Jambun Vana, Badri Vana, on top of Mahendra hills, Vindhya hills, on the banks of Godavari, in the cities of Varanasi, Mathura, Ujjaini, Dwarka, Mayapuri and Kanti[4] and many others along with their disciples have come for this Yagna[5]. They are all pure, dedicated to the Vedas, learned scholars of Vedas and are well known for their knowledge.

Upon arriving in Kurukshetra, they all took their dips in the holy waters of the *Tirthakshetra* and performed their personal rituals of the pilgrimage. Post this, they sat on the deerskins along with Rishi Bhardwaj[6]. They performed the Yagna and then started talking about different pilgrimage places they have visited. As they were exchanging stories of their journeys, Romaharshana Suta[7] – the disciple of Ved Vyasa and an orator par excellence came and joined them. Suta, as we know plays a prominent role in the telling of most of the Puranas.

So, all the Rishis turn to him and say – We have heard stories of so many Tirthas from you. Please tell us about Ayodhya – the city dear to Vishnu, his first city and the first among the Mokshadayini[8] cities of Bharat. Tell us what is Ayodhya. Who are the kings who ruled from here? What are the holy places in Ayodhya and what is their importance? What merits do pilgrims accrue from visiting them? Tell us about the nature[9] in Ayodhya, which rivers flow through it, which rivers merge here creating a holy confluence. Tell us by taking bath in them or by giving donations there what Punya or merit can one earn in Ayodhya. We are all eager to hear about this holiest of the city of Vishnu from you. Please tell us the glory of Ayodhya in the right manner.

Suta agrees and says – I learnt about Ayodhya by the grace of Ved Vyasa – the son of Parashara Muni, the knower of all Vedas, the bestower of all the knowledge, the modest sagewho is venerated by all. I bow down to him with the mantras[10] before I tell you all the mysteries and glory of Ayodhya. Listen to it with all your attention along with all your disciples. He then goes on to describe how this knowledge of Ayodhya has reached him.

In the past, Narada told it to Skanda. Skanda told it to Rishi Agastya, who in turn told it to Krishna Dwaipaiyan[11], from whom I received it. Since all of you have expressed a deep desire to listen to it, I share it with you. I bow down to Sri Ram, who has the complexion of Atasi flower[12], who is lotus eyed and is the one who killed Ravana[13].

City of Ayodhya

Ayodhya is the holiest of the cities that is inaccessible to people with bad deeds. Here lives the Hari himself in his Murti form. Who would not want to serve him? Rivalling the Amaravati of Indra, this divine Ayodhya lives on the banks of Sarayu River. Ascetics of all kinds take refuge here.

With the help of Elephants, horses, chariots and foot soldiers[14] its head is held high. The high ramparts surround the city with golden archways. It has broadroads through out the city that divide city and its parts into four squares. Huge mansions adorn its land, surrounded by impregnable walls. The city is sprinkled with ponds that are full of beautiful lotus and lily flowers. From all four directions, you hear the Vedic chants, music of the flute, veena and mridanga. Divine shrines adorn the city like jewels.

Trees of Sal, Tamaal[15], Coconut, Jackfruit, Amla[16], Mango, Kaintha[17], Ashoka etc flourish here. There are different gardens around the city. Plants here bloom in every season. Malati, Jati[18], Bakul, Patali[19], Nagchampa, Kaner and Karnikar flowers can be seen everywhere. Neem, Jambeera[20], Matulung[21], Banana are always in bloom. Nagara plants smell like sandalwood here.

Men here have divine radiance that makes them look like royal progeny and beautiful women look like celestial apsaras of the devloka. Brahmins emulate Devguru Brihaspati in intellect and poets here are par excellence. At other places, like Kalpataru[22] the residents are doing business with the traders. Horses, that look like Ucchashraiva[23] horse roam around the city. Elephants with giant tusks roam around like the guardian deities of the four directions. Full of all kind of luxuries and signs of prosperity, Ayodhya looks like the Amaravati of Indra on earth.

Ghats of Sarayu

The kings of solar dynasty, known for being dedicated to the wellbeing of their people, took birth here in the lineage of king Ikshvaku. Sarayu river, whose holy waters comes all the way from Lake Mansarovar flows here. Her banks are full of trees where the birds chirp along with the beetles. Her waters seem as if Dharma itself is flowing. It merges with the waters of Gharghara, on whose banks many Munis have their ashrams. On the banks of such sacred waters of Sarayu, Ayodhya lives.

Just like revered Ganga comes from the right toe of Vishnu, Sarayu comes from the left toe of Vishnu, making them both divine. No wonder even the devatas bow down to them. A simple dip in these rivers can absolve you of the biggest of paapa[24] like Brahmin Hatya[25].

Agastya Rishi, who was born from a pot, heard about the glory of Ayodhya from Skanda, and he came here for a pilgrimage. As per the prescribed way of pilgrimage, he bathed in the holy waters, did tarpana[26] for his ancestors, worshipped in the temples and paid homage to each holy place in Ayodhya. He felt blessed and happy when he saw the glory of Ayodhya with his own eyes. He stayed here for three nights and left Ayodhya while singing its praises. Krishna Dwaipaiyan saw him soaked in joy and bliss and asked him the reason for this state of ecstasy.

Vyasa asks what is giving you so much joy that I am feeling the happiness just by looking at your happiness. Where are you coming from?

Agastaya Rishi says that it is indeed a matter of wonder. Today I felt the sway of Ayodhya that I visited today, it is because of this city that I am feeling so much of bliss.

Vyasa says – Bhagwan, if the influence of just visiting Ayodhya is so strong, please tell me the mysteries and glory of Ayodhya in detail. What is the sequence of its Tirthas and what all Tirthas are present here, and how is one supposed to visit them? Taking bath in different kinds of Tirtha gives what kind of benefits that one can accrue? Please tell me all this in detail.

Rishi Agastya responds – You have a blessed intellect. I see that you have immense interest in listening to the glory of Ayodhya. The letter 'Aa' is Brahma, letter 'Ya' is Vishnu and letter 'Dha' is Rudra – together all three of them live in the name of Ayodhya[27]. Any kinds of sins, including the Brahmin Hatya can not reach this city. Hence, the learned ones call it Ayodhya – the one that cannot be won over.

Ayodhya is Adipuri[28] – the first city of Vishnu. It does not touch the earth as it is situated on the Sudarshan Chakra of Vishnu. Who can possibly describe this kshetra[29] where Sri Vishnu himself lives respectfully?

From Sahastradhara[30], it extends one yojana[31] towards the east and towards the west it extends for one yojana till Sam Tirtha[32]. It extends one yojana to the south of Sarayu river and as much to the north of Tamasa river. This is the extent of Ayodhya Kshetra. At the heart of this kshetra is the Antargriha or the inner chambers of the Hari. This Vishnupuri is in the shape of a fish, whose head lies in the west between Gopratar Tirtha[33] and Asita. Its tail is in the east and middle part in north and south. In this city Vishnu lives in the form of a Vigraha[34]. I have seen the impact of Ayodhya by spending time there.

Vyasa's curiosity is heightened and he asks, addressing Agastya as a tiger among the sages - You say that Srihari lives here as Vishnuhari. What is the glory of this Vishnu and how did he become famous? Describe it to me in detail.

Story of Vishnu Hari

Agastay as ays – Once upon a time, there was a noble and well-known Brahmin called Vishnu Sharma. He was expert in the Vedas, Vedangas and philosophies thereof. He used to spend all his time doing the work of Dharma, performing all the rituals, yoga and meditation. This devout Vaishnava[35] once came to Ayodhya for pilgrimage. He thought since Vishnu himself lives here; I will do tapasya[36] here. Courageous Vishnu Sharma embraced this thought and started meditating there while living only on the diet of fruits and roots.

During summers Vishnu Sharma performed his Tapa sitting in the middle of Panchagni[37]- the five fires. In the monsoon season he sat in the rains without any protection to protect him. In early winters, he stood in the waters of the lakes and performed his Tapa. He would take ritual bath and worship Vishnu. This way he brought all his Indriyas or the 5 sense organs under his control and cleansed his mind of all impurities. He balanced his Pran Vayu[38]- the inward breath and focussed completely on Vishnu. By chanting Om, he expanded and lit up the lotus in his heart. Within this lotus with the help of Sun, Moon and Agni he conceived the image of Hari in his embodied form – wearing yellow clothes, holding Shankha[39], Chakra[40] and Gada[41] in his hands. He worshiped this image with flowers and completely focussed on Vishnu. He meditated on Vishnu in the form of Brahma with the 12-syllable mantra[42], while living just on air. Three years hence passed.

After this, without any laziness in his bones, Vishnu Sharma **bowed down** to the lord of everything that is rooted and everything that moves[43], **the lord of** the universe Srihari, and sang his glory in these words:

Oh, Bhagwan Vishnu, be pleased!
Oh, best among the men, be pleased!
Oh, Devata of the Devatas, be pleased!
Oh, the lotus eyed one, be pleased!
Victory to Krishna
Victory to the one who is beyond contemplation
Victory to Vishnu
Victory to the inexhaustible
Victory to the lord of all Yagnas
Oh Vishnu, victory to the all-powerful lord of infinite
Victory to the dispeller of all sins
Victory to the slayer of the ailment of birth
I bow down to the one with lotus in his navel
I bow down to the one with lotus garland
I bow down to lord of everything including Bhootas[44] – you are the slayer of asura Kaitabh[45]
I bow down to the lord of three worlds and root cause of this world
Oh Lord of the universe, I bow down to the lord of the devatas
I bow down to the Narayana
I bow down to Krishna, Ram and the one with discus as his weapon
You are the mother of all the Lokas[46]
You are the father of the universe
You are friend of those who are in fear or distressed
You are the father and you are the grandfather
You are the offering in a Yagna
You are the Yagna done to please Devatas
You are the master of the ritual
You are the Agni that consumes everything
You are the instrument, the cause and the doer of every action
Oh, the beholder of Shankha, Chakra andGada in hands, Oh Madhava[47], absolve me from the cycle of birth and death
Oh, bearer of Mandara mountain, be pleased!
Oh, Slayer of Madhu (Asura), be pleased!
Oh, the beloved of Kamala, be pleased!
Oh Lord of the Bhuvanas[48], be pleased!

Rishi Agastya says – When Vishnu Sharma sang the glory of Vishnu with so much devotion, the soul of the universe Vishnu appeared before him, seated on his vehicle Garuda. He was attired in yellow, holding conch, discus and mace in his hands. Delighted with Vishnu Sharma, Vishnu said:

Child, I am satisfied with your intense tapasya. Oh, wise one, with the glory you sang, you are bereft of all your sins now. Oh, the Indra among the Brahmins, I am here to grant you boon. Ask your boon. Without this tapasya, no one can see me in this form.

Vishnu Sharma said: Oh, Lord of Devas, I am blessed with your embodied darshana, oh lord of the world, just bless me with the unshakable devotion in you.

Bhagwan said –Your steadfast Vaishnavi devotion will lead to liberation. Jahanavi[49], the bestower of liberation will always be present here. This place will be famous by your name.

Rishi Agastya says –After saying so, the lord of the Devatas, dug up the place with his discus and the waters of Ganga emerged from the Patala mandala. With this water, the compassionate lord removed all the dirt from that land. Vyasa, that land came to be known as Chakratirtha. This auspicious Tirtha is capable of destroying the sins of the three worlds. The one who takes a bath here and makes donations will go to the Vishnuloka.

Bhagwan again spoke to Vishnu Sharma –With your name pre-fixed to my name, a Murti will stay here at this spot. Known as Vishnuhari, it will give salvation to the devotees.

Rishi Agastya says – The wise Brahmin on hearing these words, installed a murti of the one bearing the discus at the same place by appending his name to the name of Srihari. Since then, the Vishnuhari stays here wearing yellow clothes and holding conch, discus and mace in his hands.

Its annual pilgrimage happens from the 10th day to full moon day of the bright fortnight of the month of Kartik. By taking bath at Chakratirtha, you are liberated from all your sins. Such people are honoured in the Swargloka for many thousands of years. If one performs ritual with the aim to help the ancestors and offers *Pind Dana*[50], not only are his ancestors satisfied, but they will go to the Vishnu Loka without a doubt. Those who visit the Vishnuhari after taking a dip in the Chakratirtha, all their sins are washed and they are honoured in heaven. Free from sins when you give donations as per your capability, you stay in Indra loka as long as the reign of 14 Indras[51].

On other days (of the year) as well, the ones who have gained control over their senses, can visit Chakratirtha and by looking at the Murti of Vishnuhari get rid of all their sins.

This way, the ocean of all good qualities, the one who is worth meditating on, the eternal consciousness stays here in the form of murti for the salvation of the human beings. Those who take bath in Chakratirtha and worship Vishnu with great devotion, are an embodiment of great deeds and get to dwell in the world of Vishnu.

Reference

1. Kurukshetra is better known as the battleground where the Kauravas and Pandavas fought their big battle. However, it is a region defined by the Saraswatri and Drishtavati rivers. It is one of the 4 holy places associated with four Yugas. In Satyuga, it was Naimisharanya where most of the Purana tales are based, in Treta it was Pushkar, in Dwapar it was Kurukshetra and in the present Kaliyuga it is River Ganga. Naimisharanya is considered Nimsar located about 90 km from Lucknow close to Sitapur. Kurukshetra as a town came up after 1947, the original town here was called Sthaneshwar or locally Thanesar
2. It is not clear if it is the Dashrath Putra Ram or some other Ram mentioned here. Since the Mahatmya talks about the departure of Ram, it may be another emperor named Ram. It does not even mention if it is the Ram with his capital at Ayodhya or somewhere else. Gita Press version does call him Sri Ramchandra but it too does not relate him to Ayodhya explicitly
3. Trikaldarshi
4. Kanchipuram. Note that the names of all the seven Mokshadayini cities are mentioned here indicating that they all were abodes of sages, saints and knowledgeable people
5. In one sentence the author has conveyed the extent of scared geography of India, mentioning its forests, hills, cities and rivers. He has also conveyed that learned Rishis live across the country and every 12 years they gathered at one place to share knowledge, exchange views, and if I can extrapolate it – to act as think tanks for the society and its future. They would also create strategies to take the society in the right direction or guide them. It looks like a modern-day conference where the who's who of the society are present with an intention to learn from each other, or share what they have learnt since the time they last met
6. Rishi Bhardwaj has an Ashram in Prayag
7. Hereafter referred only as Suta. Suta is both a class of people born with mixed parentage and class of storytellers who tell stories from Puranas
8. Ayodhya, Mathura, Maya (Haridwar), Kashi, Kanchi (Puram), Avantika (Ujjain) and Dwarka are considered the 7 cities that provide Moksha or the freedom from the cycle of birth and death. Ayodhya is mentioned first among these cities too
9. Ecology
10. Om Namo Bhagwate Vyasaya is the mantra he chants
11. Krishna Dwaipaiyan is another name of Ved Vyasa. Krishna because he was dark skinned, and Dwaipaiyan as he was born on an island on River Yamuna
12. Deep Blue Color of the Flax flower
13. Notice in these adjectives of Sri Ram, Suta has covered his character physically and his capabilities by one of his acts

14. The army of elephants, horses, chariots and foot soldiers put together is called Chaturangi Sena or the four types of army battalions. The size of your army is an indicator of your might. The same word gives us Shatranj – the game of chess that also involves king, queen and four types of armies
15. Palmyras
16. Gooseberry
17. Wood Apple
18. Malati and Jati are different varieties of Jasmine
19. Trumpet Flower
20. Jambeera is a type of Citron
21. Pomegranate or Sweet lime
22. A sign of abundant wealth
23. Horse that came out in Sagar Manthan or Churning of the Oceans.
24. Sins or bad merits that you accumulate with bad deeds
25. Brahmin Hatya means killing of a Brahmin, considered one of the worst sins one can commit. Even Sri Ram committed this when he killed Ravana
26. Pitritarpan is the ritual done for the wellbeing of your ancestors & all the 7 holy cities are visited to do this puja
27. Indicating that Brahma, Vishnu and Shiva live in Ayodhya all the time
28. It is also called AdiPuri as it is the first known royal city of the world, literally meaning the first city
29. Area, usually defining the sacred boundaries of a place associated with a deity
30. A central ghat located almost in the middle of the city of Ayodhya
31. A yojana = 12.87 km
32. Later described in detail as Sambhed Tirtha
33. Now known as Guptaar Ghat
34. Murti or a consecrated Statue
35. Follower of Vishnu
36. penance
37. Panchagni refers to 5 fires – four of them are lit in four direction, the meditator sits in the middle from dawn to dusk, the fifth Agni comes from the Sun. It is a considered purifying as Agni or fire cleanses everything
38. Pran Vayu is one of the five Vayus or airs that our body interacts with. These are Pran Vayu – the one which is taken in, Apaan Vayu – the one which is expelled out, Samaan Vayu – the balancing air, Udaan Vayu - the breathe moving up, Vyana Vayu that moves outward from the center of the body. Most meditation practices and Yoga requires the Sadhak to balance these 5 types of airs within the body
39. Conch Shell
40. Discus that the Vishnu holds
41. Mace
42. 'ॐ नमो भगवते वासुदेवाय'
43. जड़ चेतन
44. The 5 elements that comprise everything – Prithvi or earth, Jal or water, Agni or Fire, Akash or Sky, Vayu or Air

45. Refers to the story of Vishnu killing the Asuras Madhu and Kaitabh inside the ocean
46. Loka is a world in itself. We live in Prithvi Loka, Indra lives in Indraloka or Devloka, Brahma has his Brahma Loka, Vishnu has Vaikuntha Loka or Goloka.
47. Another name of Vishnu
48. There are 14 Bhuvanas in the Universe, you can also think of them as independent galaxies or different levels. 7 of them are considered below our earth and 7 above. Their names of 7 below are Atal, Vital, Sutal, Talatal, Mahatal, Paatal, Rasatal. 7 above are Bhuloka, Bhuvaloka, Swargloka, Maharloka, Janloka, Tapoloka, Satyaloka .
49. Another name of Ganga
50. Rice Balls are offered as part of Pind Dana
51. Each Manvantara has a reigning Indra, also known as Manu. Each Manvantara has 71 cycles of Chaturyuga or the 4 yugas. We are right now in 28th Yuga of the 7th Manvantara

Chapter 2

Brahmakund, Sahastradhara, Papmochan Tirtha and Naga Puja

Suta says that Rishi Agastya kept telling the different stories of Vishnuhari at Chakra Tirtha in Ayodhya. He says:

When Brahma, the creator of this world, came to know that Hari himself is living in Chakra Tirtha, he too landed in Ayodhya and started living here. Upon arriving he performed the pilgrimage as per norms and performed a Yagna with numerous types of offerings. Then this elder of every loka, Brahma, created a large pond and gave it his name. He invited many devatas over here. The ripples in the vast waters of this pond have the capability to remove tarnishes. It is full of water lilies and lotus flowers in white, red and blue colors. It is enchanting with swans, cranes, geese and many water birds. The trees lining the banks of this pond are full of groups of birds perching on them. Once all the devatas took bath in this pond, they were all purified and glowed with purity. The Rajas[1] in them was washed away and this surprised them all. With folded hands, full of devotion they bowed down to Brahma and asked:

Oh, the lotus seated one, tell us the glory of the pure water of this BrahmaKund! By taking bath in this pond, our rajas is removed. We are very surprised to see this. Please tell us more about it.

Brahma said–Oh surprised divine beings, listen attentively to the glory of this pond that imbibes different types of merits. By taking bath here as per the rituals, the sinful creatures get dressed in beautiful clothes, they ride the aerial chariot with swans and reach the Brahmaloka, where they live till the time of *Pralay*[2]. Oh, the best among Devatas, here sages do homa, give dana like *Tuladana*[3] and earn the merits of a *Ashwamedha Yagna*. By taking bath in this pond of mine, one is bestowed with *Sri or Lakshmi*. Anyone who takes bath here, does japa and gives charity will gain merits equivalent of big *yagnas* and all his sins would be destroyed. This excellent pond would be famous as *BrahmaKund and* I would always reside here.

On the fourteenth day of the bright fortnight of the month of Kartik, an annual pilgrimage will take place here. This will be an auspicious pilgrimage that would destroy the worst of the sins. Oh Devatas, one should donate gold and clothes as per the tradition and one's capacity to give, to satisfy the deities.

Agastaya says – After saying so, the elder of the loka, did the darshana of Chakratirtha along with the devatas and disappeared. Since then, this pond is immensely popular on earth. This great pond is situated to the east of Chakratirtha.

Rinmochana Tirtha

Suta says – After this story, the pot-born Rishi Agastya was again asked by Vyasa and he continued to tell the stories.

Agastya says – Oh fortunate one, listen to the gory of another Tirtha, that is inaccessible to anyone with bad deeds. On the banks of Sarayu is Rinmochana[4] Tirtha. It is situated in the waters of Sarayu, seven hundred dhanush[5] north east of Brahma Kund. Once upon a time, Lomansh Rishi on his pilgrimage reached here. Upon taking bath here, he was released of all his debts and sins. Upon seeing this, he was filled with delight and had moist eyes, he said to other Rishis – Great Munis, listen to the glory of this Rinmochana Tirtha. With tears of joy in his eyes and his arms raised and he thus spoke.

Lomanshsays - Known as Rinmochana, this is the best of Tirthas, where when one takes bath, in a moment all your debts are gone. It instantly frees one from all the debts accrued in this loka or in the other lokas and all the three types of debts that one carries. This is the best among all Tirthas as its merits can be seen with your own eyes. I have experienced this myself here. So, people should come here, and per their devotion and capability, they should take bath as per rituals and give donations of gold and clothes.

Paapamochana Tirtha

Agastya says – This way while singing the glory of this Tirtha, Lomansh Rishi disappeared. Now I have told you the glory of Rinmochana, where one can get rid of all their debts just by taking bath[6]. From theRinmochana Tirtha, 200 Danush eastwards in the water of Sarayu only lies Tirtha called Paapamochana. By taking bath here one gets rid of all the sins. Have no second thoughts about it, I have been a witness of its great glory.

Once in the Panchaldesh lived a Brahmin called Narhari, who fell into bad company and accumulated paapa[7]. Due to bad company, he derailed from the path of the scriptures and did many bad deeds like Brahmin hatya[8]. Once he came in touch with some pious people who were on a pilgrimage to Ayodhya. Narhari came here along with them. In the company of these good people, he also took a bath at the Paapamochana Tirtha. All his bad deeds dissolved instantly and he became free of them. Bereft of all the paapa, he was showered with flowers from the skies. He rode on a divine aerial vehicle and reached the Vishnuloka. Witnessing this big miracle, I too took this special bath with all devotion.

For getting rid of all paapa, one should specially take bath here on the fourteenth day of the dark fortnight of Magha month along with giving donations. On other days too, a bath here can remove all your paapa.

Sahastradhara Tirtha

To the east of Paapmochana Tirtha about 100 Dhanush away in the waters of Sarayu is another excellent Tirtha. It is known as Sahastradhara, and it removes all kinds of paapa. In the past, Lakshman, the destroyer of brave in opponent's army, gave up his life here using his Yog Shakti and merged back into his original form as Sheshnag.

A Dhanush measures three and a half Hasta[9]. Four Hastas form a unit of Danda.

Suta says that after listening to pot-born Agastya rishi, Krishna Dwaipaiyan asked again with curiosity. He says – Please tell me more about the glory of Sahastradhara Tirtha, my heart is not yet content with the glory of this Tirtha.

Agastya says–Oh Muni, listen attentively, I will tell the story of the impressive origin of this Sahastradhara Tirtha. Once upon a time, Raghupati Ram having finished the work of the Devatas, was in a meeting with Kaal[10]. Before starting this meeting, Kaal had put up a condition that if anyone witnesses this meeting[11] I will abdicate that person. The door of that meeting room was being guarded by Lakshman. As the meeting was in progress, the glorious and great ascetic Durvasa[12] reached there. He was famished and he spoke affectionately to Lakshman.

Durvasa said –Hey, son of Sumitra, immediately go to Ram, and tell him about my arrival. I have a special purpose to come, so it is not appropriate for you to act otherwise.

Agastya says –Scared of the curse of Durvasa, Lakshman went inside, stood before Ram and said – Son of Atri, the one bestowed with the wealth of Tapa, Rishi Durvasa is here to see you. On hearing this, Ram sent off Kaal and came out of the room. He bowed down to Rishi Durvasa and personally fed him with his hands before sending him off. Scared of not keeping his own vow, he abandoned Lakshman. Lakshman too aware of the fact that he has violated the words of his elder brother, quickly proceeds to banks of river Sarayu. He took a bath there and sat down to meditate. He calmed his mind and focused it on the eternal consciousness. There appeared the thousand hooded king of serpents by piercing the ground from below. On the other hands, Indra came from Devloka with all his devatas (to witness this). In front of all the devata, Indra spoke to the Lakshman who had merged with the soul of Shesha – the serpent.

Indra said– Get up, Oh, Lakshman and rise up to your position. You have done the work of devatas by slaying the enemies. May you attain the best and eternal place among the Vaishnavas. Now, please get up and enter your place. Your timeless form of Shesha has come here with its hoods. He has come here by piercing the earth with his thousand hoods. The precious mani[13] in their hoods have burnt thousand holes here. So, this place located on the banks of Sarayu from now on will be known as auspicious Maha Tirtha Sahastradhara, there is no doubt about it. Extent of this area would be twenty-five Dhanush. One who takes bath here, gives donation and respectfully performs shraddh[14] for his ancestors here he will get rid of all his paapa, become pure consciousness and proceed to Vishnuloka. So, people should take bath here as per the rituals. They should see the image of Sheshnaag in the Brahmins they worship.

Gold, grains and clothes should be donated here after performing the rituals for ancestors with devotion. Taking bath, giving donations and by performing worship of Vishnu here, one becomes indestructible and loses nothing. This great Tirtha bestows everything one desires for; it happens and there are no second thoughts about it.

On the fifth day of bright fortnight of Shravan month, good people should worship the Sheshnag and organize a grand festival for the Nagas or serpents. When a festival is celebrated for serpents with devotion and Brahmins are contented, the hooded serpents are pleased and they do not trouble the human beings.

Those who take bath here in the month of Vaishakh with a pure heart, they do not have to take a re-birth for one crore[15] Kalpas[16]. So, humans should make an effort to take bath, make donations and worship the Hari as well as the Brahmins. The one who does so at this Tirtha, all his desires are fulfilled.

Lakshman merging back with Sheshnag at Sahastradhara

A person who with the aim of Vishnu, donates a milk giving cow decorated with jewelry along with her calf to a Brahmin, he gets to live in Vishnuloka forever. A bath here makes one enjoy eternal bliss in Swargaloka. In the month of Vaishakh, for the affection of Lakshmi-Narayana, and specially for gaining Lakshmi[17], one should adorn a Brahmin couple by offering garlands and clothes. In the month of Vaishakh, all the Tirthas of the world congregate here. They live here for the whole of the month, there is no doubt in this. That is why taking bath here in the month of Vaishakh is special, as taking bath here is like taking bath in all the Tirthas.

Agastya says – Oh Muni, after saying so, Indra installed Sesha, who is capable of removing the weight of this earth at this Tirtha. He made Lakshman ride his aerial chariot and himself proceeded to his Devloka. This Tirtha holds a special relevance in the month of Vaishakh. It is most beneficial on the 5th day of bright fortnight of Shravan month. Apart from this, taking bath at Sahastradhara on any festival day or an auspicious day, makes one eligible for Swargaloka. The wise men who take bath here, make donations as per the prescriptions and as per their capability, they become free of bad influences and enjoy all the pleasures of life. After death they attain Sayujjaya Mukti[18] with the Ramapati or Vishnu who sleeps on the Sheshnag.

Reference

1. Rajas is one of three Gunas – Sattva, Rajas & Tamas. Rajas is the action, the property that pushes us to act, often depicted by red color
2. Dissolution, when everything is dissolved back into Brahman, a time between two cycles of creation
3. Tuladana is a type of donation where one donates things equivalent to one's weight. Most of the times grains and food items are donated, but there are mentions of kings giving gold worth their weight. In the famous Rukmini Satyabhama story, Rukmini weighed Krishna with a single leaf of Tulsi against all the wealth of Satyabhama that could not equal the weight of Krishna
4. The one that gives liberation from debts. As per scriptures there are three types of debts – Dev Rin – the debt we owe to the devatas, Pitri Rin – the debt we owe to our ancestors including our parents and Guru Rin – the debt we owe to our teachers
5. Dhanush is a measure of length approximately 1.6 meters
6. Sometimes there is a lot of repetition of the same words. Lomansh Rishi said the same thing, and then Agastya Rishi repeats it, and for us actually Suta is repeating it. In a way, it reinforces the importance of the Tirtha and it also carries the endorsement of each person who is vouching for it, making it important for the listeners or readers to go and visit this Tirtha

7. Account of bad deeds, sometimes called sin but may not exactly mean that
8. Brahmin Hatya or Killing of a Brahmin is considered worst of the sins
9. Roughly 0.5 meters
10. Kaal refers to time. Here it would mean the deity representing time.
11. Indicating that it was a secret meeting that no one else should have access to this discussion. Accounts also say that this was the meeting to decide the time of Sri Ram leaving earth and hence a complete secrecy was required
12. Rishi Durvasa is notorious for being short tempered
13. Precious gemstone that some serpents are believed to have in their hoods
14. Ritual for departed ancestors
15. A crore = 10 Million
16. One Kalpa is a day in the life of Brahma = 4320 Million human years
17. Lakshmi means prosperity and fortune of all kinds
18. There are different types of Mukti or freedom from cycle of birth and death. Salokaya – where you get to live in the same world as Vishnu, Sarupya – where you become like him in all possible ways, Samipya – where you get to live closer to him and Sayujjaya – where you merge with him and become one in a way that you are inseparable from him. The last one is irreversible and hence the ultimate goal of all devotees.

Chapter 3

Swargdwara & Chandrahari

Suta says – On hearing this dialogue between Narada and pot-born Agastya, Krishna Dwaipayan spoke in sweet words:

Vyasa says – Bhagwan, excellent glory of this Tirtha is amazing. By listening it from you, my heart is ecstatic with joy. My heart is not yet content with the stories you tell, please continue telling the glory of other Tirthas, so that I can listen.

Swargdwara

Agastya says –Oh Brahmin, let me tell you about another glorious Tirtha. Known by the name of Swargdwara[1], it removes all the paapa. No one can say the glory of this Tirtha in great detail, so listen to it in brief. Towards the east of Sahastradhara, this Tirtha extends to 636 dhanush in the waters of Sarayu, this is how the scholars who know Puranas define it. There was no Tirtha like Swargdwara in the past nor will any happen in the future[2]. I say this again and again and again, trust me I tell you the truth that there is no Tirtha that can parallel Swargdwara in the whole cosmos. All the divine and earthly Tirthas leave their own places and come to Swargdwara every morning[3]. So, anyone who wishes to get the benefit of bath in all the Tirthas should take a bath at Swargdwara early morning before the sunrise.

Those living beings who leave their bodies[4] here at Swargdwara, find a place near Hari, there is no doubt about it. See, this Swargdwara is the door to liberation and attainment of Swarga, hence this best of Tirtha earned its name Swargdwara. This Swargdwara is not easy to get even for devatas. Whatever one wishes for here, he definitely gets all that. Highest of the Siddhis and tallest of the goals can be achieved here. The benefits of doing japa, dana, homa, darshana, tapa, meditation, study etc here last forever, they never go waste. All the paapa accumulated over thousands of previous births vanish the moment you step foot in Swargdwara.

Brahmins, Kshatriyas, Vaishyas, Shudras, those of mixed varnas, worms, those who do not follow Vedic dharma[6] and even those born in lower Paapayoni forms like insects, ants, animals and birds when they die at Swargdwara get the benefits of holding Kaumauduki[5] in their hands and will ride on the Garuda[7] to auspicious Vishnuloka. Men will become like Vishnu and live in his Loka. Whether one goes to Swargdwara with a wish in one's heart or without a wish, if you die here, you get a place of honor in Vishnuloka.

Muni, Devata, Siddhas, Sadhus, Yakshas, Marutas – all come to Swargdwara. They use one length of their Yagnopavit or the scared thread to mark their own personal space for meditation. Devatas come here at noon, so they all take a bath at noon with utter respect. Those who have learnt to control their senses, if they fast here or live here for a month they find themselves in the best possible places. Those who donate grains, gemstones, land, cow and clothes to the Brahmins, get to go to the realm of Hari.

From here, Siddhas, Great souls, Munis and ancestors all go to Swarga, that is why this place is called Swargdwara. Hari himself as Raghuram, split himself into four parts[8] and lived here with his brothers. Four faced Brahma gives up his Brahmaloka, and along with other devatas, he lives here eternally. Resident of Kailash, Shiva also lives here. Even the paapa as tall as Mandar mountain or Meru mountain get absolved here. The benefits of the next life that one gets by doing tapa, yagna and spending time in gaining knowledge all life is received by just dying here. Rishi, Devas and even Asuras perform homa here. Yati[9] and those willing of Artha or Moksha engage themselves in serving here.

The benefits that one gets by living in Kashi for sixty thousand years, during the Kaliyug, one will get it in less than half a second in this Dashrath's city of Ayodhya. Merely by talking bath here on the day of Hari[10], one accrues the same merits that yogis get by giving up their lives in Varanasi. The one who dies at Swargdwara never gets to see the hell. By the grace of Keshava, they gain the best path possible for them. Of all the divine Tirthas that are present on this earth or anywhere in the cosmos, this Tirtha is the best among all of them, oh learned Brahmin.

Those who have devoted themselves to the Bhakti of Vishnu and firmly enjoy it, those who have given up their interest in the mundane everyday subjects and have focussed all their energy by all means in their tapasya, they will not take birth for millions of Kalpas. A learned man even when attacked with hundreds of weapons chooses to stay at Swargdwara, as by staying here one transitions to the next world without any repentance. It does not matter if one leaves the body during

Uttarayan[11] or Dakshinayan[12], here there is no difference between these two times. All the times are auspicious for the one who takes refuge at Swargdwara. Just by taking bath here, all the sins are dissolved, no matter how many sins one has accumulated with their bodies. Scriptures also mention this respectfully that for people like these Ayodhya is the greatest abode.

Chandrahari

During the bright fortnight of Jyeshtha month, and especially on the full moon day, devatas come for the annual pilgrimage of Chandra Hari Deity. Yogis who have taken a Chandrasahastravrat[13] do the Udayapan[14] of their vow on the full moon day. This Vrat gives the benefit of best of Yagnas, so one should make an effort to observe this Vrat.

Vyasa says – Bhagwan, tell me the auspicious origins of Chandrahari and the ritual to observe this Chandravarat till its Udayapan.

Agastya says – Moon, the treasure trove of nectar, bowed down to the Vishnu who lives in Ayodhya,as soon as he arrived here with his curiosity to see glory of the Tirtha by himself. After this he followed the norms of the pilgrimage and was awestruck after visiting different Tirthas. He did a tough penance[15] to please Vishnu. After pleasing Vishnu, he installed a Murti of Vishnu by pre-fixing his own name with it. This is how this Murti came to be known as Chandra Hari.

By the grace of Vasudev, this place became wonderful. Oh Sage, know this as the most secret and sacred abode of Vasudev. It is the bestower of liberation on all living beings. Sidhhas always come here with the intention to do Govindvrat[16]. With a desire of Vishnuloka in their hearts, they take different forms and hold different icons. These yogis who have won over their senses, and have liberated souls practice the ultimate forms of Yoga here. The merits that one earns here can't be earned elsewhere. The donations, austerities and yagnas performed here never lose their value for the doer. All the living being attain all that they desire and wish for here. That is why one should make all efforts to give the charity and worship the Brahmins, especially worshipping the Brahmin couple is very fruitful here. All the merits that you get by doing all kinds of yagnas, visiting all possible Tirthas in the world, doing darshana[17] of all devatas in the universe, one gets the same merit by mere darshana of this Tirtha. That is why the scriptures like Puranas call it a Mahakshetra or the holiest of the sacred regions.

ChandrasahastraVrat

People should first observe the Chandrasahastravrat and then do its udayapan or formal completion of the vrat with the help of a Brahmin. To calculate when to perform the Udayapan of this vrat, understand this. After every two years, eight months, seventeen days and one-eight of a day, comes Adhik Masa[18]. As per the solar calendar, one completes witnessing of 1000 moons in life at the age of eighty-three years and four months. However, if you count using the lunar months, it comes a lot earlier. So, one should take into account the solar counting only. If one lives to be 83 years and 4 months, one should come here and perform Udayapan of ChandrasahastraVrat.

The merit that one gets by continuously engaging in yagnas, by always speaking the truth and by donating gold, or by those who live a thousand years, the same merit is gained by those who perform the ChandrasahastraVrat when they have seen the thousand moons.

On the fourteenth day, clean your teeth and have bath. With your heart, speech and body follow the norms of Brahmacharya[19]. Next day, on the full moon day, do the worship of moon, followed by worship of mother goddesses or Devis like Gauri and others. Then, perform the Vriddhi shraddh and worship the Ritiviks[20]. Then one should create the murtis of the moon. One thousand Murtis are recommended. Depending on one's capability it can be half of that, or even half of half of that or even less depending on the means available. Minimum of sixteen murtis[21] should be made as per the norms mentioned in the shastras. Each of these Murti should precisely weigh 16 Masa[22]. They should then be worshipped as per the Agama Shastras.

Then, one should perform the homa with Soma[23] Mantra as per one's financial capability. While chanting the Soma mantra one should install the murtis created, and then chant the story of birth of Soma followed by Somsukta and then perform the worship of Moon as per Agama Shastras. After this Chandra Nyasa and Kala Nyasa[24] should be performed with water placed at prescribed places. Nyasa of eleven sense organs[25] should also be performed. The Chandra mandala[26] should be replicated with white rice and in the middle a pot full of white milk should be kept. Four full pots should be kept in the four corners of the square that forms this mandala. This mandala should then be worshipped with the following names in a serial order :

Himanshu[27] Namah
Somchandra Namah
Chandra Namah
Vidhu Namah
Kumud Bandhu[28] Namah
Soma Namah
Sudhanshu[29] Namah
Aushadhisha[30] Namah
Abja[31] Namah
Mrigank[32] Namah
Kalanidhi[33] Namah
Nakshatranath[34] Namah
Sharvarinath[35] Namah
Jaivatirika[36] Namah
Dwijraj[37] Namah
Chandrama Namah

One by One, with these sixteen names, one should praise the moon. Devotee should then take water in a conch shell and offer it to Moon along with flowers, fruits, sandalwood paste and chant this Mantra:

'Oh Shashanka[38], at the end of every month, you are reborn again and again. Along with Rohini[39], please accept my offerings. This way, after performing the worship of moon with devotion, for attaining peace for oneself, devotee should offer 16 other pots full of milk that are covered with cloths and gemstones to the Brahmins. After this, do ablutions with water mixed with milk and finally satisfy all the Brahmins to the best of your ability. Organize a feast to feed all the Brahmins along with their families. Post this, a Brahmin couple should be worshipped with required efforts by means of offering clothes. They should be given ample and best of Dana and Dakshina[40]. The Murtis made for the ritual should be given to the Brahmins along with gold, silver, clothes and specially the grains with a happy heart for the love of moon devata. After this the devotee should stay on Upvasa or fast for the rest of the day. Next day after worshipping the devatas, one should sit with his family and eat food to complete the ritual. By performing this Chandravrat, one can absolve oneself of even worst of sins like killing of a Brahmin, consuming alcohol, theft or having an affair with one's Guru's wife. He becomes pure and gets to go to Chandraloka. Whatever a person may be, after doing this vrata he becomes dear to Narayana. Blessed is the one who performs this every day.

Reference

1. Literally – the door to heaven
2. Meaning it holds the importance for eternity
3. Pratah Kaal – the time just before sunrise
4. Means die
5. Malechha is usually translated to barbarians or followers of other religions.
6. Name of the mace of Sri Vishnu
7. Vehicle of Sri Vishnu
8. Ram, Lakshman, Bharat, Shatrughan are believed to be four parts in which Vishnu split himself.
9. Jain Monks. Ayodhya is also home to many Jain Tirthankaras including the first one – Adinath
10. Ekadashi or the eleventh day of every fortnight which is considered a special day by followers of Vishnu
11. Uttarayan or North Transit is 6 months of the year when Sun travels from south to north or from the zodiac of Capricorn to Gemini. Of the six seasons in India, three of them i.e Shishir (Winters), Vasant (Spring) and Grishma (Summers) fall during this time. It is usually considered auspicious half of the year. Famously Bhishma in Mahabharat chose to wait for his death till Uttarayan sets in
12. Dakshinayan or South Transit is 6 months of the year when Sun travels from north to south or from zodiacs of Cancer to Sagittarius. Three seasons within this are Varsha or monsoons, Sharad and Hemant or early winters
13. Chandrasahastra translates to 1000 moons that would be roughly 83 years and 4 months.
14. A closing ritual to formerly complete a vow that you have taken
15. Tapashcharan – a tapa done for a pre-ordained number of Japas, usually considered very difficult and not many people can do it
16. Vrat involves chanting and meditating on the 'Om Namo Bhagwate Vasudevayah Namah' mantra
17. Visiting a temple is essentially to do darshana of devata, literally it means looking at the God or witnessing the God, but the word communicates far more than just looking at the deity, it includes the connotation of communicating with them and establishing a connect with them, and through them with ourselves
18. Adhik Maas or 'The extra month' is calculated to re-align the lunar and solar calendars. Lunar months have 28 days while solar months have an average of 30.42 days. So, after 2 years, 8 months, 17 days and part of a day, an extra month is added. This month is known by various names like Adhik Maas, Mal Maas or Purushottam Maas. It is dedicated to doing lot of religious activities including some of the pilgrimages. Here the calculation of one's age to decide when one should perform the rituals for Chandrasahastra Vrat is explained
19. Norms of Brahmacharya include not hurting anyone, not indulging in any Tamasic activities like eating bad food, arguments or wishing anyone bad even in your thoughts, observing celibacy. One is supposed to keep the behaviour Satvik so that you can put all your energy in the task at hand - the rituals of Vrata in this case.

20. Ritiviks are people who perform Yagnas as per norms in Vedas, that might include sacrificial yagnas as well.
21. Moon has 16 Kalas or 16 phases that represent a fortnight or a Paksha. A Matrika or a goddess is associated with each of these 16 tithis
22. Unit of Weight, 1 Masa = .972 grams and 12 Masas form a Tola, a unit that was used to measure precious metals in India
23. Another name for Moon, that is how we get the name Somvar for Monday
24. Nyasa is the mental consecration of the deity being worshiped in one's body and mind.
25. Five Gyana Indriya – Eyes, Ear, Nose, Skin, Tongue and 5 Karma Indriyas – Hands, Feet, Anus, Penis and Speech, 11th - Mind
26. A geometric representation of the deities
27. One with cooling rays
28. Related to water lilies
29. One with nectar like rays
30. Rulers of the medicines
31. Born of water
32. One with a deer in his lap
33. One whose treasure is the Kala or the parts that form the dates
34. Lord of the Nakshatras or constellations
35. Lord of the night
36. One with long life
37. King among the Brahmins
38. One with hare in his lap – referring to the mark on the moon that looks like as if a hare is sitting on it
39. Rohini is one of the 27 Nakshatras, considered one of the favorite wives of Moon
40. Dana is donation that you give as charity, Dakshina is a fee that you give for helping you do the Puja. Dana is your choice while Dakshina is the right of someone who performs rituals on your behalf

Chapter 4

Dharmahari & Swarnkhani

Dharmahari

Agastya says - Towards the South East[1] of this Chandrahari is another deity called Dharmahari, who can destroy all the sins collected in Kaliyuga. Once upon a time, a Brahmin called Dharma, who was well versed in Vedas and Vedangas, who was known for his dedication and sincerity towards his work, came here for pilgrimage. He performed the extensive pilgrimage with all devotion and he was awe-struck by the unparalleled glory of the Tirthas of Ayodhya. Delighted with joy, he raised his arms in ecstasy and said – 'How beautiful is this Tirtha and how excellent is its glory'. I have never seen a city like Ayodhya, that does not touch the ground but sits on the Chakra of Vishnu. Hari himself lives here, how can any other city ever be compared to this city. Every Tirtha here is capable of giving you a place in Vishnuloka. This is the great Tirtha of Vishnu, this is the great city of Ayodhya, its glory is incomparable. What here is not worthy of worship and praise? After saying so, Dharma broke into dancing in various ways with the delight that came from realising the special glory of Ayodhya city.

Witnessing the Dharma dancing with pure ecstasy, yellow robed Vishnu himself appeared before him. Dharma bowed down to him, and with great respect spoke this Stuti[2]:

> Namah to the one who dwells in the ocean of milk–the Ksheersagar
> Namah to one who lies on the bed of Shesha–Sheshashayee
> Namah to the one whose feet are touched even by Shankara
> Namah to the one whose lotus feet are worshipped by the devotees
> Namah to the one who is dear to Brahma and other Devatas
> Namah to the Madhav who has auspicious body and beautiful eyes
> Namah to the one with lotus feet

Namah to the one with lotus in his navel
Namah to the one whose feet are touched by the waters of the ocean of milk
Namah to the one who bears Sharang[3] in his hands
Namah to the one whose sleep is yoga
Namah to the one who is meditated upon by the best of Yogis
Namah to the one who rides the Garuda
Namah to the one called Govinda
Namah to the discus holder, one with beautiful hair, nose and forehead
Namah to Sridhar[4] who wears beautiful clothes and has lovely complexion
Namah to the one with mighty arms
Namah to the one with pleasing thighs
Namah to the one with beautiful residence
Namah to the one who is most divine
Namah to the one who has all the Vidyas[5]
Namah to the one holding the mace
Namah to Keshava
Namah to the one who is most peaceful
Namah to the one who took the form of Vamana
Namah to the one who adorns yellow robes
Namah to the one who upholds the Dharma

Agastya says –The lord of the world, the lord of the Sri, Hrishikesha[6] pleased after listening to his Stutisung by Dharma, thus spoke:

Bhagwan said–Oh Dharma, I am really content with this Stuti of yours. Oh Dharmagyay[7], ask me for a boon for whatever is dear to your heart and mind. Whoever will sing this Stuti of mine, without any lethargy and with full concentration, he will get all that he wishes for, he will be immensely respected and prosperity will always stay with him.

Dharma said – Oh Lord of the lords, if you are pleased with me, I would like to install you here with my name attached to yours.

Agastya says –'So be it' said the Bhagwan and he transformed into Dharmahari. By merely thinking of Dharmahari Murti, one is liberated. One who takes bath in the waters of Sarayu river with good thoughts in his mind and takes the darshana of Dharmahari, he gets rid of all his paapa. Giving grains in donation, doing japa, homa and feeding the Brahmins here yield merits that stay forever and the devotee gets a place in Vishnuloka. One should perform rituals as described in the scriptures to dispel the bad impacts of any deeds done knowingly or unknowingly. Only by performing proper rituals can one get rid of the sins; hence one should make an explicit effort to do the same. Knowingly or unknowingly if there is a break in performing the daily rituals prescribed, may be due to the royal orders[8] or other reasons, or if one is under some stress, the repentance rituals should be performed carefully. Here Vishnu Dev himself dwells with affection, who can ever have the capability to describe the glory of this place.

Oh Brahmin, on the Ekadashi or the 11th day of the bright fortnight of Ashadh month, one should do the annual pilgrimage of this Tirtha. One should take bath in the Sarayu at Swargdwara and then do the darshana of Dharmahari. By doing so, one gets rid of all paapa and becomes pure soul and gets to live in Vishnuloka forever.

Gold Mine

To the south of this (Swargdwara), there is a best of gold mine. This is where Kuber, afraid of Raghu, caused a rainfall of gold coins.

Vyasa says – Bhagwan, why did Kuber cause the downpour of gold here? Why was he afraid of Raghu? Tell me all this in detail. My mind will not be content till I listen to this mysterious story.

Agastya says –Listen Oh Brahmin, I will tell you this beautiful story of the origin of goldmine. Most humans are greatly surprised when they listen to this story. Once upon a time, Raghupati–with whom the dynasty of Ikshvaku flourished, ruled the whole earth with his kindness, vigour and the immense power of his own arms. His enemies though envied his reputation, even then they sang praises of the ways in which he ruled the world. Raghu took refuge in the best of policies to rule and protect his subjects. The rays of the glow of his fame and popularity illuminated all the ten directions. By means of his military conquests he accumulated a lot of riches. He attacked different countries with his mighty Chaturangi Sena[9], brought them under his control and collected taxes and tributes. Illustrious and powerful king Raghu brought all kings under him with his prowess and this is how he accumulated riches including different type of gems and precious stones. After collecting all these riches from all possible directions, he came back to Ayodhya – his splendid auspicious capital. Once in Ayodhya, this descendant of Kakutstha[10] became eager to perform a Yagna. With pure mind, he decided to perform a Yagna befitting his family traditions.

The courteous king called his advisor Muni Vasishtha, and through him he invited Vamadeva, Kashyap Rishi and all the other excellent Munis living in different Tirthas. Watching them arrive looked like coming together of pure Agni or the blazing fire from everywhere. Raghu, the conqueror of many cities of the others, the descendant of Kakutstha, came out of his quarters and with great humbleness spoke to the gathering of excellent Munis with aim of achieving the desired merits from the Yagna:

Raghu said – All the Munis who have come here, please listen to me. I wish to perform a yagna, please give me the permission to do so. As of now I have wished only this much. Which Yagna is appropriate for me, please discuss among yourself and direct me accordingly.

Munis said – Oh King, there is a Yagna named 'Vishwajit[11], excellent among the Yagna. You should perform this immediately with all possible efforts, without causing any delay.

Agasyta says – Then, the king collected all the material things[12] like sweets required for the Yagna and performed the Vishwajit Yagna. He donated everything he had in Dakshina as part of this Yagna. The munis participating in his Yagna were content with the ample donations they received. With great regards, king gave away everything he had. All Munis content with the respect and donations they and their families received, returned to their own abodes. Upon the successful completion of the Yagna, from that very moment, the king became even more resplendent like the lord of the devas - Indra in the Swarga.

In the meantime, there came Kautsa Muni, who lived with Vishwamitra in his inner quarters[13] and was well known for his self-control. He came with an intention to sanctify Raghu and ask for donation that he can in turn pay to his Guru. Kautsa Rishi respectfully begged the king for gold coins. He said – 'When I repeatedly asked my Guru for the Dakshina I should pay him, in anger he said, go get me fourteen crore gold coins'. King Raghu had already donated everything as part of the Yagna. Despite this he got up from his seat and welcomed Kautsa Muni and worshipped him with great respect. By this time Raghu was left with only a clay pot, which he used to perform welcome rituals for Kautsa Muni. Looking at the clay pot, Kautsa Muni was surprised and lost all the happiness in his heart. He gave up the hope of receiving the Dakshina. Well versed in the use of right words, Kautsa Muni spoke these sweet words :

Kautsasaid – Oh King, may you prosper. You have given up everything in this Yagna. You are devoid of any riches now, so I will not ask you for money. Now, I will goelse where to seek Dakshina for my Guru.

Agastya says – After the Kautsa Muni said so, Raghu – the conqueror of enemies, thought for a moment and then with folded hands he spoke with utter politeness.

Raghu said –Bhagwan, please stay in my palace for a day. In the meantime, I will make an effort to get the money you have asked for.

Agastya says – After saying these very generous words to the Muni, Raghu left with an aim of conquering Kubera. When Raghu reached Kuber's place, upon hearing of his arrival, Kuber pleased Raghu by showering gold in his kingdom. The place where it rained gold, became the best of goldmine[14]. Raghu showed this gold mine to Kautsa Muni and dedicated all of it to him. Muni respectfully took the gold he needed to pay his Guru and returned the rest to the king. The wise muni blessed the king with many boons.

Kautsa said –Oh King, you will beget a very illustrious son who will possess all the great qualities of your dynasty. This gold mine will bestow upon you all that you desire in your heart. This will be a great Tirtha that will take away any sins of anyone who takes bath here and makes donations.He will gain all the prosperity. On the twelfth day of the bright fortnight of month of Vaishakh will be the annual pilgrimage yatra of this Tirtha. As per my words, anyone who comes to this Tirtha would get all their different desires fulfilled.

Agastya says – This way content with his heart's desire fulfilled, Kautsa Muni blessed the king enthusiastically. As per his plan, he left for his Guru's ashram. King too was satisfied and he distributed the rest of the gold among the Brahmins and went back to protecting his people. This is how the glory of Swarnakhani was created due to Kautsa Muni.

Reference

1. Agneya Kona or the direction of Fire God Agni
2. Stuti are verses said in praise of someone
3. Name of Vishnu's bow
4. One who holds the Lakshmi or the consort of Lakshmi
5. Knowledge in different fields
6. One with hair as illustrious as the rays of Sun and Moon, also the one who has won over all his senses

7. One who knows the path of Dharma
8. Would mean Government orders in our day and time or obligatory duties towards the state
9. Chaturangi Sena is fourfold army consisting of elephants, horses, chariots and foot soldiers
10. Another mighty king of Suryavansha who ruled from Ayodhya, one of the predecessors of Raghu
11. Literally meaning – World Conquer
12. Collectively called 'Dravay'
13. Referring to him being a close and dear disciple of Vishwamitra
14. Swarnkhani is how this place is known

Chapter 5

Kautsa Story, Sambhed Tirtha, Tilodaki

Vyasa says – Please tell me why did Rishi Vishwamitra in his anger ask his disciple Kautsa for such an (huge) amount of Dakshina that is very difficult to get even with best of efforts. If you have any graciousness towards me, please tell me about this in detail.

Agastya says – Oh Brahmin, listen to this story by concentrating all your senses on it. Vishwamitra is best among the Munis and the possessor of divine vision. Once he was engrossed in a tough penance with all purity as per his vow. One day Durvasa Muni came there with the purpose of the darshana of Vishwamitra. As soon as he entered, he spoke loudly – I am suffering from hunger pangs, please give me food. Immediately give me some warm Payasam[1] so that my hunger goes away. Listening to these words of Durvasa, Vishwamitra got up and with great efforts put the Payasam in a plate and offered it to Durvasa Muni. On seeing him standing with the Payasam, Durvasa Rishi who is known for his quick wit, spoke these sweet words – 'Oh Best among the Brahmins, please wait for few moments. Now I am going to have my bath, till I come back you please sit here and wait. Do sit and wait for me'.

After saying so, Rishi Durvasa left for his own ashram. Vishwamitra stood right there like an immovable mountain waiting for him. Even after a thousand divine years passed, he stood steady in body and mind. Rishi Kautsa who is very generous and without any envy in him, took upon himself to serve and take care of Vishwamitra. After a while, devoid of any bad deeds, Rishi Durvasa came, ate the Payasam and went back to his own hermitage. After he left, the mine of Tapa, Vishwamitra asked the best among the learned Kautsa Rishi to return to his own home[2]. Being discharged of his duties, Kautsa Rishi asked his Guru – What Dakshina should I pay you?

Vishwamitra said – What Dakshina will you give? You have served me enough and that is your Dakshina. Now you leave for your own home, oh dedicated Brahmin.

The disciple though kept repeating his request, and this annoyed Vishwamitra. In anger he said these harsh words – 'Get me fourteen crore gold coins in Dakshina, and only after that you go home'.

Agastya says - Upon listening to this order from his Guru, Kautsa muni deliberated a bit and then decided to approach Raghu, the conqueror of the all direction and descendant of Kakutstha to ask for Dakshina.

This is the answer to your question, now listen to the story of another excellent Tirtha.

Sambhed Tirtha, Tilodaki

To the south of Swarnkhani is a Sambhed Tirtha that is served by many Siddhas. This is also the confluence of Tilodaki river and Sarayu river, well known in the world. By taking bath here, one becomes Viraja or without the Rajas Guna[3]. The merits that you accrue by doing ten Ashwamedha Yagnas, the same merits are accrued by a righteous souled person taking bath here.

The one who donates gold etc to the learned Brahmins well versed in Vedas achieve the auspicious salvation.He becomes resplendent like the glow of pure fire. Whoever gives food as donation here at the world-famous confluence of Sarayu and Tilodaki River, never has to take birth again on this earth. The one who fasts and satisfies the Brahmins by giving them food, he gets the merits of performing Sautramani Yagya[4]. The one who lives on one meal a day for a month here, he gets rid of all the sins done in this life. On the Amavasya or no moon day of Nabhasya or Bhadrapad month is the annual festival of this Tirtha. Oh Brahmin, in the good old days, Ram had created this river like another Sindhu[5] River for the drinking water of the horses acquired from Sindhudesha[6]. Since the pious waters of this rivers were dark like black sesame seeds[7], it came to be known as Tilodaki. If a person takes bath in Tilodaki river, even at places other than the confluence, he becomes bereft of the sins accumulated over seven births.

Oh Muni, anyone who wishes to earn the merits of Dharma, they should make all efforts to visit Tilodaki and have a bath in her waters, make donations, perform vrata and homa to gain unending merit. This way, one who goes on different pilgrimages as prescribed, his personality improves, his good qualities enhance and he earns merits. The one who worships Hari with all the devotion in his heart at all these Tirthas, all his sins disappear somehow and he attains the ultimate abode of Hari.

Reference

1. Rice and Milk pudding, also known as Kheer in North India
2. This could mean return to Grihstha ashram or the life of a householder instead of a renunciate
3. As per Indian traditions, we all carry different Gunas within us – Satva, Rajas & Tamas. Satva is the pure part, Rajas is the action-oriented part responsible for our actions, Tamas is the laziness and lethargy that makes us dormant. The balance of these gunas is what is recommended. At lot of places, you take bath or perform some rituals to let go of your need to take action and move towards the Satva Guna. The Shaktipeeth in Odisha is called Biraja meaning the Devi is without any Rajas Guna and is pure Satva Guna.
4. Also known as Indrayaag
5. Indus River thar originates from Ladakh in India but mostly flows through Pakistan now
6. Sindh Province
7. Til in Hindi and Sanskrit

Chapter 6

SitaKund, Guptahari, Goprataar Tirtha, Sarayu Gharghara Sangam, Departure of Sri Ram

Sitakund

Agastya says - To the west of confluence of Tilodaki and Sarayu, on the banks of Sarayu is famous Sitakund. It is well known for bestowing devotees with all the wishes. By taking bath in it, all the sins go away. Sita herself had created this kund[1]. With the boons bestowed by Sri Ram, this pond has become the treasure chest of all the merits one can collect.

Sri Ram said –Listen Sita, I will tell you the glory of this kund of yours. Oh, fortunate one, I am telling this story for your affection. Oh, the one with mild and pure smile, anyone who takes bath here, donates, performs japa and homa, his merits earned will never dissipate. Specially on the fourteenth day of the dark fortnight of Margashirsh[2] month when one takes a bath here all the paapa gets dissolved.

This is the boon that Sri Ram, the favorite of his subjects, gave to Sita. Since then, this Tirtha has become world famous and came to be known as Sitakund. Visitors find it magnificent. Anyone who takes bath here will definitely attain Ram. Bathing, donating and meditating is important here. By doing worship of Sri Ram along with Sita, especially when done with fragrance, flower garlands, incense, lamp etc as per one's capacity, one will be liberated from the cycle of birth and death, there is no doubt in it. If you take bath in the month of Margashirsh, you will never have to take birth in a womb again, but taking bath at any other time too will take you to Vishnulok.

Chakra Tirtha, Guptahari & Goptratara Tirtha

To the west of Sitakund, on the banks of Sarayu lies the bestower of all desired merits, Chakrahari Tirtha of Vishnuhari. Oh Brahmin, the glory of this Chakrahari can never be told, not even the best among the wise and patient can ever describe. To the west of it is holy tirtha called Harismriti. This sacred land of Vishnu bestows the best of merits. Even by the mere sight or darshana of this tirtha, all the sins are washed away. By looking at these two tirthas, all the bodily sins burn away and the sins done on the earth just perish.

Once upon a time there was terrible battle fought between the Devas and Asuras. Devas were defeated by the Asuras who were bubbling with the pride due to a boon they had. Devas had to leave the place. While fleeing away, their leader Hara[3] stopped them from running away and took them to the shores of the Ocean of Milk[4] to meet the Vishnu sleeping on the bed of serpents.

There Devas saw the Vishnu lying on the bed of Shesha in the ocean of milk, with his lotus feet in the hands of Lakshmi sitting next to him. Narada and other munis sang praises of great qualities of Vishnu. Garuda sitting in the front was singing his stuti uninterruptedly with folded hands. Waves of ocean were leaving their marks with the drops of water on his garments. Stars like the grains of sand, shine like a garland of pearls around him. He is wearing yellow garments. He wears an eternal smile on his face, that is full of emotion of kind delight. He wears large earrings in both his ears that are full of resplendent pearls. A creeper goes around him studded with the gems and jewels found in Shwetadweepa[5]. His crown has a band of bright Rubies going around it. His radiance of the Kaustubh Mani[6] on his chest produces a halo in deep red colorthat can dispel the fear of Rahu in Sun[7] .It appeared as if he is contemplating the creation of another four-faced lord[8].

At such a time, with humility in his mind, Shiva came there singing his eulogies in all his modesty. He was accompanied by the group of Devas who took refuge in Vishnu - the conqueror of all the enemies of the Devas, by singing his stuti.

Ishwara said –

Namah Oh Hari, you take us across the ocean that this world is, you are the one who gives happiness to Garuda[9], you are the moon that dispels the darkness of Moha or delusion.

I take refuge in the knowledge in the form of a lustrous jewel, in mind that is like moonlight and in the devotion to the lord that is like a river flowing through the gardens of our mind.

It is the power of your enthusiasm that pervades through all the three worlds. Along with your Vaishnavi[10] Shakti you created the millions of species and living beings since eternity.

For all those who are about to fall just like the petals of a lotus losing their stability when faced with violent storms, the only way to attain stability is Hari Smriti – remembering the name of the Hari.

Namah to the Sun like soul, whose knowledge radiates like the rays of the Sun. These rays of knowledge only are responsible for opening up the petals of the glorious lotus in our hearts.

Namah, you are the perpetual goal of all the Yogis who follow all the Yamas[11]. Your kingdom lies beyond the realms of lights and darkness.

Namah, you are the Yagna, you are the offering offered in the Yagna and in the form of three Vedas – Rig, Yajur and Sama, it is you. Namah to the one whose good qualities are constantly praised in the songs sung by the Saraswati.

Namah, you are the quiet, the storehouse of dharma, soul and nature of the nectar, you show your disciples the path of yoga, the reason behind the living beings, you appear in formidable form created using your Maya, I bow down to you with thousand heads.

Namah to the soul who is sleeping in Yognidra[12], from the flower in your navel Brahma the creator of the universe takes birth, to the one who lives in the world in the form of water – the very reason for the sustenance of the world.

Namah, you are the one who can only be experienced through the effects of your works, you are present both in the Jiva[13] and Atma[14], you are the protector of the Pranavayu that is vital for the living beings, I bow down to that soul of the universe with all my devotion.

Namah to the one who takes the form of a glorious lion to vanquish the daityas[15], one who cannot be known within the limits of our mind or capability, the one who bears the load of all the universe.

Ignorance is the reason for this world to exist and only you are capable of dispelling this ignorance. You live in the secret space that is beyond the realms of our contemplation. Namah, to you who is also Rudra.

You are the one who quietens the waves inside our mind and take us to Kaivalya Pada[16]. Namah to the one who is bereft of all the emotions and yet lives equally inside each one.

I bow down to you, who has the complexion of a blue lotus, who has the lustrous hair shining away, who wears the Kaustubh Mani, who is like an elixir to the eyes looking at him.

Agastya says –Hari with Garuda emblem, who easily gives boons, was delighted to hear this Stuti from Shankara. He threw his nectar filled gaze on the group of Devas present there, who bowed down to him. Then, he spoke to them with these sweet words:

Bhagwan said – Oh Devas, I know the reason of your coming here by way of my Samadhi[17]. You are terrified by the attacks of powerful daityas who are full of pride and have snatched away your position. Those with greater strength only can conquer the ones with less strength. So, now I will perform the Tapa to gain strength for all of you. I will go to the city of Ayodhya and perform the supreme Tapa. I will be present there secretly or in unmanifest form to increase your strength and brilliance so that you can pacify the daityas. You too, without any impurities in your mind quickly head to Ayodhya and perform the severe Tapa for vanquishing the daityas.

Agastya says – After saying so, Hari with the Garuda emblem, disappeared from there. Soon after, he arrived in Ayodhya and started performing the severe penance. As he performed the Tapa in a Gupta[18] state for strengthening the devas, here he came to knownas Guptahari. Upon arrival, the place where the Sudarshan Chakra fell off from the hands of the Hari came to be known as Chakrahari. A mere glance at these places liberates one form all the sins. By the effect of the tapa of Hari, Devas gained strength. They won over all the daityas in the battle and gained back their positions. They were immensely delighted after defeating the asuras.

After this all of them along with the Brihaspati[19], came to visit Hari in Ayodhya. They bowed their heads to the lotus feet of Hari and his feet became adorned with the garlands they were wearing. Upon arrival they attentively listened to the different stutis being sung in praise of Hari. With folded hands they worshipped him with complete devotion and focussed their mind to meditate on him with all allegiance. On seeing them thus soaked in his devotion, the yellow robed Janardana[20], the soul of this universe, spoke with affection.

Bhagwan said – Oh Devas, I am seeing you after a long time by some play of destiny. Now, tell me which wishes of yours should I fulfil? Tell me without any fear and do not delay saying it.

Devas said –Hey Bhagwan, hey lord of the lords, hey lord of the world, all our tasks have been fulfilled because of you. Even so, to protect us always, please stay here forever. We pray to you that with control on all sensory organs, protect us by always destroying our enemies.

Bhagwan says –I shall do so. I will stay here and help you conquer your enemies. I will grow the brilliance of the Suras[21] who are endowed with Sri[22]. This excellent story will gain fame in all the lokas. My name Guptahari will be famous in the world. This secret place of mine will now be well known in the world. Here anyone who worships me, performs puja, yagna and japa etc with complete devotion to me, will reach the desired destination. Anyone who gives donations here as per their capacity to give, with all their senses under control, he will attain the unparalleled position in Swargaloka.

Those desirous of getting righteous merits, for my affection they should make an effort to donate a cow along with a calf as per the norms. The cow should have her horns covered in gold and her hoofs should be covered in silver. She should be dressed up with two pieces of clothes. A copper vessel to collect her milk should be given along. This cow with many qualities should have her back in rust red color of the copper. Her tails should be adorned with precious stones, and a beautiful bell should adorn in her neck. She should be worshipped using the garlands of fragrant flowers. She should be a happy cow, none of whose calves are dead.

The cow should be given to a deserving Brahmin with good qualities, who is well versed in Vedas, is without any impurities in his soul, is a Vishnu devotee, a respected scholar and who is kind and compassionate. Donating a cow to such a Brahmin[23] gives happiness to everyone – meaning both the donor and the receiver. One should not donate to just any Brahmin, as it will cause the downfall of the donor. One who donates to gain my affection, also should do so with no impurities in their heart. He should take bath here with an intent to let go off all the impurities, they will proceed to Swarga and attain Mukti easily as if it was just lying on their palms.

To gain my affection, one should make efforts to give donations and do japa and homa at this Chakrahari Tirtha of mine. Oh Devas, you all should also do the pilgrimage here as per the norms. Near my Guptahari Tirtha, there is a holy confluence. To the west of Goptratara it lies about three yojana, where the river named Gharghara merges with the Sarayu. Here,take a bath as prescribed and then you should do the darshana of Guptahari, who bestows the fulfilment of all your desires.

Agastya says –After saying so, the yellow-robed Achyut[24] disappeared. Devatas after performing the pilgrimage, soaked in the devotion for Hari, started living in Ayodhya. Oh, best of Brahmins, since then the place has become famous on this earth. The annual pilgrimage of the Guptahari happens on the full moon day of

Kartik month. After taking bath at Goptratara Tirtha, and at the confluence of Sarayu and Ghaghra, one should worship Guptahari, he fulfils all the desires. Also, one should visit the Chakratirtha in the month of Margashirsh, during its bright fortnight and on the favorite date of the Hari which is Ekadashi or the eleventh, to attain a place in Vishnuloka.

Sutasays – After saying so the pot-born Agastya Muni stayed quiet. Krishnadwaipayan Vyasa again spoke with curiosity.

Sarayu Gharghara Sangam

Vyasa says –You have told me this amazing story, oh Taponidhi[25]. My mind is full of surprise now. Tell me the wonderful glory of this Sangama in more details.

Agastya says – Oh eminent Brahmin, listen to the glory of this wonderful confluence. I will tell you the story of this Sangam as I heard it from Skanda Dev. I gathered from Skanda Dev that eleven thousand crore tirthas perpetually live at the confluence of Sarayu and Gharghara. This includes Devatas, Suras, Siddhas, Yogis as well as Brahma, Vishnu and Shiva, who always stay close by. Listen, Oh, learned Brahmin, let me tell you the merits gained by taking bath in the confluence with a focussed mind, doing the shraddh for one's ancestors, giving donations as per one's capability and doing homa with Vaishnava Mantra. Here you get the same merits as you get by doing thousand Ashwamedha Yagnas, hundred Vajpayee Yagnas or by donating gold at the great Kurukshetra tirtha on the day when Rahu engulfs the Sun[26].

Taking bath here on the no moon day, full moon day, twelfth day of each fortnight, on the day of Ayana[27] and during Vyatipat Yoga[28] makes one attain the Vishnuloka. The merits that one gets by performing severe penance by standing on one foot for thousands of yuga[29] can be gained easily by taking a bath at this confluence on the full moon day of Pausha month as per the norms.If one hangs oneself upside down for ten thousand yugas to perform penance, the same benefit can be gained by taking bath in the pure waters of this confluence. The benefit that one gains by taking bath here cannot be gained by doing hundreds of Yagnas. The bath taken during the Paushamonth is particularly beneficial. Whoever takes bath here in the month Pausha, be it a Brahmin, a Kshatriya, a Vaishya, a Shudra or one with mixed lineage, he goes to the Brahmaloka and is restricted from coming back on earth.

Listen to the merits accrued by the one who offers a lamp of ghee during the month of Pausha. Big or small sins earned over different lifetimes; they all dissolve away, just like salt dissolves in water. One who offers ghee lamp every day on this Tirtha will get long life, health, prosperity, the joy of having children along with accruing merits. The one who fasts on the thirteenth day of the bright half of Pausha month and performs Jagran by keeping awake whole night, he goes to the mansion of Hari or Vaikunthaloka.

Let me tell you the rules of the Jagran. After lighting the lamps everywhere, one should engage a learned Brahmin who has his sense under control, to perform a yagna. After performing the Vishnu worship, one should listen to the story of the Vishnu and please Vishnu by singing and dancing with music. This way one should spend the night listening to the meritorious stories of the Vishnu through the night. In the morning, one should take bath as per the norms, perform the worship of Vishnu and donate gold etc to the Brahmins as per one's capability. The one who donates gold, food, clothes with pure devotion at the confluence as per the established norms, he attains the ultimate goal in life. People engaged in doing meritorious works should do this Jagran year after year. When one satisfies the Brahmins engaged in the worship of Hari as per one's capability, the Vishnu is pleased with them. All their sins fail to hurt them just like the poison of a serpent fails at the sight of Garuda bird. One who takes bath here goes to heaven, the one who takes bath here leads a happy life. All the living beings in the three worlds, when they perform tarpana, attain the ultimate satisfaction courtesy the waters of the holy confluence.

For all the living beings seeking relief from the miseries of life, there is no better place for them to go, other than this confluence. One who takes bath here not only redeems himself but also seven generations preceding and seven generations succeeding him. The one who comes here and does not takes bath and prays at the confluence of Sarayu and Gharghara, is as good as those who are born blind and lame. This Tirtha stands tall among all the tirthas just like Brahmins among different *varnas*[30]. The one standing at the confluence of Sarayu and Gharghara is comparable to the one who lives in the abode of Vishnu. Here anyone who takes bath and gives donation as per his capacity with all his senses subdued, performs homa as per prescriptions, he is bound to go to Swarga. Whether it is a man or a woman, they all should take bath here as prescribed, they will definitely find a place in Swargaloka, there is no doubt in this. Just like fire burns everything, be it wet or dry, same way this confluence reduces all your sins to ashes. If the merits offered by all the other tirthas are weighed against the merits offered by confluence of Sarayu and Gharghara, the latter would weigh far more. The merits that the scriptures tell us of visiting all possible tirthas can be attained just taking a bath at this confluence.

Goptratara Tirtha

Oh Anagh[31], close to the confluence lies another great Tirtha called Gopratara which all destroys the biggest of the sins. The one who takes bath here and makes donations will never be struck with grief of any kind. There has been no tirtha at par with Gopratara in the past and will not be there in the future either. Just like the learned people talk about Manikarnika in Varanasi, or Mahakaal temple in Ujjaini, just like there is unforgettable Chakravapi at Naimisharanya, the same way Ayodhya has the great Gopratara Tirtha. Here, with the permission of Sri Ram, the residents of Saket[32], took bath and attained bliss in heaven.

Vyasa says – How did the residents of Saket go to Swarga? How did Ram himself go to heaven. Tell me all this, oh Suvrata[33]!

Agastya says – Oh Muni, listen to this attentively, I will tell you in detail, how did Ram, along with the people of his city go to Swarga. In the old days, Sri Ram having completed the task of the devatas with all efforts, decided to proceed to Swarga along with his two brothers[34]. Vanaras[35] who could change their form as per their wishes learnt about his departure and came there. They were followed by Rksh[36], Gopuchh[37] and Rakshasas[38], who came jumping along. Devatas and sons of Gandharvas[39], Rishis and Vanaras too upon hearing about Ram's departure, approached Ram. The leaders of the groups of Vanaras asked –We have all come to follow you. Oh, bull among the men, if you leave this earth to go to your Dham, without taking us along, we will anyway be dead due to the huge punishment of the pain of separation from you.

On hearing these words of Rkshs, Vanaras and Rakshasas, he (Sri Ram) immediately spoke to Vibhishana[40]- 'As long as there are people in this loka, till then you rule the great kingdom of yours in Lanka. Treat your people righteously. Do not think of my words otherwise and there is no need to reply to me on this topic.'

After saying this to Vibhishana, the descendant of Kakutstha, Ram turned to Hanuman and spoke – 'Oh, son of the wind, you have to lead an eternal life. Do not waste this vow. Till people keep retelling my story, you have to sustain this vow of yours. Mainda and Dvivida[41] have both experienced the nectar, they too will live forever till the end of the three worlds. You protect my sons and grandsons here'. After saying this, Raghav, the descendant of Kakutstha spoke to rest of the Vanaras – 'All of you come with me'.

When the night made way for the dawn, broad-chested Ram who had great arms and eyes in the shape of lotus petals, spoke to his purohit[42] - 'Let all sacred fires of all the Agnihotra, Vajpaaye and other sacred fires go ahead of me'. The brilliant Vasishta muni understanding the decision of Ram, as per the norm started preparing for the rites for the mahaprasthan or the ultimate departure of Sri Ram from earth.

Ready for his mahaprasthan, Sri Ram adorned Kshom[43] clothes like a brahmachari and held Kusha grass in both his hands. The king said no auspicious or inauspicious words. Just like moon emerges from the ocean, he came out of the city of Ayodhya. On the left side of Ram, Sri along with her lotus joined him, and on the right the wide eyed Hrim[44] joined him after arriving there. Different types of weapons like bow and bow string too took the human form and started following the Kakutstha Ram. Vedas took the form of Brahmins and walked to his left, and Savitri walked to his right. Likes of Omkar and Vashatkar[45] also started following him. All the rishis, mahatmas and mountains also started walking along with Ram and reached Swargdwara. All the women from the inner palace of the descendant of Kakutstha, including the old women, young girls, servants, ministers and the doorkeepers followed him. Along with the people of inner apartments, Bharat and Shatrughan too stepped out. Leaving everything behind, Ram walked ahead and everyone from Raghu's lineage followed him. The great Brahmins along with all their Agnihotras, their sons and their wives too started following the Kakutstha Ram. All the ministers along with their servants, sons and kinsmen started going where Raghav Ram was going. All the nature along with hale and hearty people started following the footsteps of Raghav, the mine of good qualities. All the subjects of the city along with their children and families left behind all their sins and started following Ram. They all took bath with a focussed mind and wore white clothes, and the sound of their joyous squeaks filled the atmosphere. No one there was dejected, afraid or unhappy. Everyone was happy, joyful and full of curiosity.

With a desire to witness the Nirvana, the kings of the different kingdoms arrived via the aerial route. Bears, monkeys, rakshasas and all the residents of the city with great devotion started following him. This city was bereft of any living beings as they all reached Swragdwar following Raghav. All those mobile and immobile beings, when they looked at Kakutstha Ram, a desire to go to the Swarga

Sri Ram going to Sarayu

took birth in them. There was not even the smallest of living beings in Ayodhya, who did not follow Ram and who was not present at Swargdwara.

After this Ram walked about half a yojana and turned west for the darshana of the holy waters of Sarayu. At the same time, the grandfather of this loka or Brahma along with all the devatas and sages came to the Kakutstha Ram present at Swargdwara. All around him there were millions of divine aerial vehicles in all directions illuminating the place with their brilliance. The sky was illuminated with the brilliance of all the bright great souls with holy deeds present there. Pleasant, mild and fragrant breeze was flowing. Gust of wind led to the windfall of flowers from the skies. Apsaras and Gandharvas worshiped the Sun God present there. After this Ram touched the waters of Sarayu with his feet and devatas led by Brahma started singing his stuti.

Brahma said - Hey Dev, you are the lord of all the lokas, who can ever know you. Of large eyed one, in the past, I emerged from you only. Oh, lord with great vigour, to sustain these lokas you who is eternal, unimaginable and unconceivable has taken many wonderful forms in different bodies.

After listening to these words of Brahma, the lord entered the divine and radiant world of Vishnu along with his brothers. There in the body of Vishnu, all the devatas worshipped him as the best among them. Sadhus, Maruts, Agni and other primary Devatas, divine Rishis, Apsaras, Gandharvas, Suparna, Nagas, Yakshas, Daityas, Danavas, Rakshasas are all delighted with their desires fulfilled. All the residents of Devaloka in Swarga say – Sadhu Sadhu[46].

Then the radiant Vishnu spoke to Brahma – Oh Suvrat[47], to all these people, give the best possible lokas. They have all come with me for the affection they have for me. They are my devotees, completely devoted to me and they have left behind everything for me.

On hearing these words of Vishnu, lord of all worlds Brahma spoke – All these people will go to the loka named Santanika. Whoever leaves his body, meditating on the name of Ram, here at the Swargdwara, will attain the Santanikloka that is beyond the Brahmaloka. Vanaras will go back to their yoni[48], Rakshasas will go to Rakshasa yoni, whoever came from whatever body will gain the same one. Sugriva, the son of the Sun will enter the solar system. Rishis, Nagas and Yakshas will go back to their origins.

After saying so, lord of Devas, Brahma reached Gopratara tirtha that is a part of the waters of Sarayu only. All the people entered the waters and gave up their bodies. After leaving the humanly bodies they all boarded the divine aerial chariots. The beings of Tiryak yoni[49] also entered the Sarayu waters. They left their earthly bodies and entered their divine bodies. Other mobile and immobile creatures too attained the divine body and they left for Devaloka. After all this, the bears, vanaras and rakshasas too entered the water and left their bodies, and remembering the lord they entered the heaven. Ram too along with the Devas happily left for the heaven.

Oh Brahmin, since then, this tirtha is known as Gopratara Tirtha. No other tirtha is at par with this tirtha that gives the ultimate liberation from cycle of birth and death. As a result of the good deeds over hundreds of births, if one comes to Gopratara Tirtha, he gets liberated in one life only. There is no doubt that Hari lives here always, that is why here in one life only one can achieve Moksha. Any man, learned or otherwise, who takes bath here with total faith, achieves the place that is difficult even for the Yogis to access. Specially, on the full moon day of Kartik month, all those who have their senses under control should come and take bath here. During the month of Kartik, all the devatas come to Ayodhya to take bath in Ayodhya. A tirtha like Gopratara has never happened in the past, nor will one happen in the future.

Prayag, the king of Tirthas, where wishing for good deeds one gets rid of all sins, one's body becomes pure and glows, that same Prayagraj also comes to take a bath in this Tirtha in the month of Kartik. All possible holy places on the earth, all of them come to Gopratara tirtha in Kartik month. All the japa, homa and dana performed at Gopratara when done with faith and by following the vows, gets you the merits that stay with you forever. During the Kartik month, all Tirthas say – let's go to Gopratara Tirtha to get rid of all the sins we have accumulated.

All the sins are destroyed by taking bath in Goptratara Tirtha. One who takes bath here and then takes the darshana of Guptahari, without a doubt he becomes free of all his sins. Specially, one should worship the Brahmins with an aim to achieve the Vishnu. One should take bath with devotion, following one's vows, one should offer a milk yielding cow along with all the ornaments to a Brahmin who is well versed in Vedas and who dutifully follows all the rules and conducts all the rituals as prescribed. He should be pure and his soul always focussed on the affection of Sri Vishnu. To attain the devotion for Hari, one should donate different types of grains, gold and clothes here. The merits that one gets by doing Tulabhara dana at Kurukshetra during solar eclipse and on Narmada during lunar eclipse, the same merits one gets by lighting a lamp here. Oh lion among the Munis, the one who lights a lamp of ghee or sesame oil here, what more gain can he get from doing anAshwamedha Yagna!

The one who lights a lamp in front of Keshava during the month of Kartik, has performed all possible rituals to be done at a Tirtha. All the different types of tirthas that promise the worldly pleasures as well as liberation are not even worth the one-sixteenth part of the Gopratara Tirtha. Anyone who donates even a small amount of gold to a Brahmin well versed in Vedas, will shine with brilliance just like fire. Oh Brahmin, Gopratara Tirtha is well known in the three worlds, anyone who donates grains or food here as per the norms, need not fear a rebirth. Anyone who after taking bath here, satisfies the Brahmins with his donations, gains merits worth performs a Sautramani Yagna.

Anyone who lives here for a month eating just one meal a day, observing all the norms and vows, all his bad deeds collected during this life are destroyed. Oh, the wealth of Tapa, one who enters the fire here, he is bound to get status of Vishnu, there is no doubt in this. Those who take an indefinite fast here with devotion to Vishnu, they will not take rebirth on earth for millions of Kalpas.

One who worships Govind here at Gopratara, he gets the merits comparable to donation of ten gold coins. Offering incense to Govinda is worth anAgnihotra Yagna, and offering fragrance is akin to donating land. This place has been called very wonderful by all the learned people in their glories. A bath during Kartik month is specially purifying here. The one who takes bath at Swargdwara will gain merit worth donating ten gold coins, and the one who donates gold here with devotion will get a place in Swarga.

One should perform Jagran or night long worship here on the fourteenth day of the bright fortnight of Jyeshtha month. Doing it on Parvani[50] days at this excellent tirtha will yield merits worth donating gold. After finishing this, one should purify oneself by taking bath and then worshipping the Vishnu and making efforts to light lamps, to accrue different types of merits.

The merits of the three worlds i.e. Swarga, Martaya[51] and Rasatal only make noise till one offers a lamp on the waters in front of Keshav[52] during the Kartik month.

On the morning of full moon day, one should take bath with a pure heart and mind, and perform the worship of Hari as per norms and do shraddh[53] with due respect and devotion. One should donate food as per one's capacity to satisfy the Brahmins, and donate clothes and ornaments after worshiping a Brahmin couple. One should then do the darshana of Bhagwan Guptahari and particularly worship him by bowing down to him at his tirtha with a pure mind. At noon time, one should take bath at Swargdwara as per the rituals. By doing so, one becomes devoid of paapa and proceeds to Vishnuloka.

Thus, whoever follows all the rules as prescribed to take bath here and worship the beautifully made Murti (of Hari), all his sins go away. By worshipping Achyut, he becomes devoid of all the impurities and becomes one with Vishnu by merging with him[54].

Reference

1. Pond
2. Also known as Agahan
3. Shiva
4. Ksheersagar
5. Mentioned in Mahabharata Shanti Parva as an island located north of Ksheersagar, where the fair complexioned people live, who are pure and smell good always
6. The 4th of the 14 jewels that came out during the churning of oceans between devas and asuras
7. Rahu is the cause of solar eclipse and in poetic terms it has the capacity to engulf the Sun or the reason for the Sun to be afraid of Rahu
8. Brahma, who in turn is responsible for rest of the creation
9. Suparna is the name used for Garuda here
10. Shakti of Vishnu
11. Yamas are practices like non-violence, not telling a lie, not stealing, letting go of greed and celibacy
12. Yogic sleep
13. Individual living being
14. Ultimate being from which all other beings emanate
15. Sons of Diti, usually against the devas, reference here is Narasimha Avatar
16. Ultimate seclusion that takes you away from the cycle of birth and death
17. A state of meditation
18. Hidden
19. Brihaspati is Dev Guru or the Guru of all Devatas
20. Another name of Vishnu
21. Devas
22. Lakshmi
23. Indian texts repeatedly talk about the 'Supatra' or the right recipient for any donation
24. Another name of Vishnu
25. One whose wealth is Tapa
26. The day of solar eclipse. Bathing in Kurukshetra during a solar eclipse is a pilgrimage in itself

27. The day Sun changes it path from North to South or South to North i.e., the day it enters the zodiac of Cancer and Capricorn
28. An astrological calculation that is considered malefic and related to calamities
29. A yuga consists of thousands of human years
30. Brahmin, Kshatriya, Vaishya, Shudra are the four varnas based on the different professional activities performed within a society
31. Sinless
32. Another name of Ayodhya
33. The one who engages in good holy rites
34. Bharat and Shatrughan. Lakshman has already gone back to his loka at Sahastradhara already described in Ayodhya Mahatmya.
35. Monkeys
36. Bear as well as Seven Rishis
37. Cowherds
38. Asuras or demons
39. Celestial beings
40. Younger brother of Ravana and the designated king of Lanka
41. Two Vanaras who were a part of Vanara Sena and are supposed to the sons of Ashwin Kumars
42. Rishi Vasishtha was the Purohit of Sri Ram
43. Some people interpret it as silk clothes and others as clothes made from leaves. I would go with the latter given the situation
44. A form of Devi in which she is the supreme Brahman
45. The mantra spoken while making an offering to the yagna fire
46. An expression of delight meaning excellent
47. Someone who has undertaken many good Vratas or vows
48. Species
49. Species of small living beings like worms, flies, insects, germs
50. Days on which moon changes i.e. new moon, full moon, fourteenth and eight of every half of the month
51. Earth
52. Implying that the merits of lighting a lamp in front of Keshav is more than all the merits of three worlds put together.
53. Rituals for ancestors
54. Sayujjya Mukti

Chapter 7
Stories of Different Ponds in Ayodhya

Ksheerodaka

Agastya says - I will tell you about another Tirtha known as Ksheerodaka. Full of good qualities, it is situated in the north-west direction from Sitakund. It is the abode of many merits and it is the destroyer of all kinds of miseries. Once in the past, king Dashratha very respectfully performed a Putreshti[1] Yagna here, as per its prescriptions, with a desire to beget a son. After the completion of the Yagna, with lot of joy he gave away ample dakshina. At the end of the Yagna, the one who receives the offerings of the Yagna[2] appeared in the embodied form. He was holding a beautiful golden vessel full of Havish[3] in his hand. That Havish had the refulgence of Vishnu enshrined in it. The king divided that Havish into four parts[4] and gave it to his wives.

Due to the attainment of that very difficult to get Ksheer[5] here, this place came to be known as Ksheerodaka. It destroys all the sins. Surrounded by water on all sides it bestows best of merits. The one who is learned and has his senses under control takes a bath here with reverence, all his desires are fulfilled and he gets wise and famous sons. On the eleventh day of the bright half of Ashwin month, with senses under control, one should take bath here as per the norms and donate to the Brahmins as per one's capacity. By worshipping Brahmins as Vishnu here with all the prescribed norms, all the desires one has, are fulfilled. He will beget many sons and his merits will grow with time.

Brihaspati Kund

To the south-west of the Khseerodaka lies the famous Brihaspati Kund full of fierce and powerful beings. The nectar like waves of this kund are destroyers of all the sins. Guru of the devatas[6] himself lives here. Ever generous Brihaspati performed a yagna here as per the norms. This beautiful place is full of the qualities of many Munis and shade of many leafy trees. This kund is inaccessible for the sinners. Indra and other devatas also make an effort to take a bath here to get the desires of their hearts fulfilled and to gain beauty and generosity. Human beings get rid of their sins after taking a bath here and making donations.

A pilgrimage here on the fifth day of the bright half of Bhadrapada month is extremely meritorious. On the other occasions too, a bath here on Thursdays bestows merits. The one who performs the worship of Brihaspati along with Vishnu here, he gets rid of all his bad deeds and enjoys the Vishnuloka.

The ones with Jupiter afflicted in their Gochar[7], should take bath in this kund as per the established rituals with a sankalpa[8]. Such a person should perform a yagna and get a murti of Brihaspati made in gold. He should wrap it in yellow cloth and while standing in the water give it to a Brahmin who is pure and is well versed in Vedas for the purpose of getting relief from the pains of affliction. One should do the homa along with the japa for the planet (Jupiter). By doing so, there is no doubt that the pain caused by the affliction of the planet will be relieved.

Rukmini Kund

Oh! best among the Munis, to the south of it is excellent Rukmini Kund. It was built by Rukmini Devi, the beloved of the Krishna, herself. Vishnu himself stays in the water here. Out of his love for his wife, he gave her this boon, adding to the importance of this place. Here one should take bath, make donations and do homa with Vishnu Mantra, and then worship the Brahmin and the Vishnu with sincere efforts.

One should also make an effort to participate in the annual pilgrimage here on the ninth day of the dark half of Kartik month to get rid of all the accumulated sins. By participating in this annual pilgrimage here, even the impotent person gets sons, hence, be it a man or a woman, one should respectfully take bath in this kund. By doing so, one enjoys all the pleasures of life and then goes to Vishnuloka. Ones who seek prosperity and wealth should particularly take bath here. All of wishes come true for the ones who take bath here. One should donate as per one's capability for the affection of Rukmini and Shripati.

One should worship the Brahmins as prescribed and meditate on the lord of Lakshmi, who is holding the conch shell, discus and mace in his hands, wearing the yellow garments and garlands. He is being praised by the Narada and other munis. He is riding his vehicle Garuda; his crown is adorned by Mahendra and others and his chest is adorned with the all wish fulfilling Kaustubh Mani. He wears the complexion of the Atasi[9] flowers and his eyes are pure like the lotus flower. One who meditates on this, will have all his desires fulfilled. He will enjoy all the pleasures of this life and after that enjoy the Vishnuloka.

Dhana Yaksha

Now I will tell you about another Tirtha that takes away all the sins. It destroys all the sins and problems associated with the Kaliyuga. Highly sacred, unparalleled and bestower of all wishes, this devotion inspiring tirtha is well known as Danyaksha or Dhana Yaksha. This auspicious place is situated to the north-west of Rukmini Kund. Enormous wealth of saint-king Harishchandra was placed here. A formidable Yaksha was positioned here to protect it.

In the past Muni Vishwamitra had defeated the king Harishchandra, who was the performer of many Rajsuya Yagnas. He got hold of all his kingdom including his Chaturangi forces consisting of horses, elephants, chariots and soldiers. Muni then appointed the Yaksha to take care of all his wealth. There is a temple named Pramanthur there, which gives joy and happiness. Yaksha used to live here and protect the wealth with all his efforts. Satisfied with his services, the Muni who had won over all his senses, spoke these sweet words to him.

Vishwamitra said – Oh the follower of Dharma, ask me for a boon while staying devoid of any greed. I am particularly delighted to see your absolute devotion.

Yaksha said–Oh Brahmin, if you want to grant me a wish and if you are pleased with me, please make my body smell sweet. Due to an earlier curse by a king, my body emanates foul smell. Do this if you are pleased with me.

Agastya says –When Yaksha spoke this, Muni closed his eyes to meditate and focussed on the devotion of the Yaksha. He performed the sankalpa, and poured the water of the Tirtha on Yaksha. Instantly, the body of Yaksha became fragrant. Polite and wise Yaksha thus transformed, stood with his hands folded and he spoke repeatedly in these sweet words:

Yaksha said–Oh Brave one, with your grace my body has become fragrant. Oh, Brahmin Rishi, do something that this place becomes well known to everyone. Please make an effort to make it so.

Agastya says – On hearing this, the Muni thought for a moment with his eyes closed. Pleased with the Yaksha, he spoke in a gentle manner :

Vishwamitra said– This place will attain the unparalleled fame. It will be well known tirtha as Dhana Yaksha. This place will bestow beauty upon the body. One who takes bath here with norms, will get rid of any foul smell in the body. Those who wish to earn merits should make an effort to take a bath here. One should give donations as per one's devotion and capability,then particularly perform the worship of Lakshmi. One should take bath and make donations here just for the affection of Lakshmi. One should also worship the nine nidhi[10] (s) with vows, to enjoy the pleasures of this world and to stay happily in the next world too. The nine nidhis are – Mahapadma, Padma, Shankha, Makar, Kachhapa, Mukund, Kunda, Leela and Kharva[11]. All these treasures will also stay here in this kund. Worshipping them particularly will yield many benefits. Worship of the Nidhis along with Lakshmi should be performed in the middle of the water. Different types of food grains and clothes should be given away. Gold should be given as per one's financial capability but without being miserly. One should make an effort to keep the donations secret[12]. Fruits and gold should be particularly donated.

A bath here on the fourteenth day of the dark half of the month is very beneficial. It should be done with great devotion by the one who has complete faith in this place. On the fourteenth day of dark half of Magha month is the annual pilgrimage for this, when one should take bath here and perform the rituals for the ancestors. One should say -'May everything from a small blade of grass to Brahma, all be satisfied' and offer three handfuls of water with the sacred thread worn over right shoulder. By doing so, one will never get caught in the illusions. One who takes bath here becomes divine, the one who takes bath here always lives happily. Those who take bath here must first perform worship for you (Dhana Yaksha). With your worship all their sins will dissolve away. 'NamahPrathamrajah' will be your mantra. Your worship and shravana[13] shall be performed in the middle of the water.

In this Tirtha, Nidhi, Lakshmi and your worship is of importance. One who performs these with patience, all his desires will be fulfilled. The one who wants wealth will get wealth, one who wants sons will get sons, one who wants salvation will get salvation, what is that one cannot receive from here. Hey Yakhsa, anyone who out of delusion does not take bath here, you will take away a year's worth of all their merits.

After giving these boons, Vishwamitra Muni, the one with the wealth of Tapa, disappeared from there. Since then, this Tirtha has gained fame. All the land in this Tirtha is covered with gold. It is studded with divine jewels whose radiance lightens up all the directions. Anyone who serves this place, gets all his goals fulfilled.

Vasishtha Kund

To the North direction of Dhana Yaksha is situated the famous Vasishtha Kund, that is known to remove all kinds of sins. The storehouse of tapa, Vasishtha Muni always lives here in this Kund, as does the Arundhati[14] who is always engaged in doing rituals with complete purity. A wise person gains the best of merits by taking bath here and by performing the shraddh or rituals for one's ancestors.

Vaamdeva[15] also lives here in this Tirtha, so one should worship both Vasishtha and Vaamdeva here. Arundhati who is devoted to her husband must be specially worshipped here. One should take bath as per the rituals and donate as per one's capacity to give. All your desires are fulfilled here, there is no doubt about it. The one who takes bath here becomes like Vasishtha.

On the fifth day of the bright half of the month of Bhadrapada, one should do the annual pilgrimage here as prescribed. One should make an effort to do the Vishnu worship here with complete devotion. By doing so one becomes pure and devoid of all sins, and gets honoured in the Vishnuloka.

Sagar Kund

Oh, Indra among the Brahmins, to the west of VasishthaKund lies the famous Sagar Kund, the bestower of all desires. One who takes bath here and gives donations, gets all his desires fulfilled. The merits that one gains by taking bath in the sea on a full moon day can be gained here by taking bath on the Parvani days here. One who is desirous of begetting a son, should take a bath here specially on the full moon day of the month of Ashwin.By doing so, all the sins go away. By taking bath here, and by making donations here as per one's capability, one gets to go to the heaven.

Yogini Kund

To the south west of Sagar Kund is the excellent Yogini Kund, where the sixty-four yoginis live inside the water. It gives all kinds of benefits to everyone, but especially to women. Yoginis bestow all kinds of Siddhis[16], and fulfil all kinds of desires.On the eighth day of the bright half of Ashwin month specially, one should make an effort to take bath here to please the Yoginis. Taking bath here and giving donations brings all kinds of successes. With the influence of Yakshinis, you get all Siddhis, there is no doubt about that.

Urvashi Kund

To the east of Yogini Kund is the excellent Urvashi Kund. One who takes bath here will attain the Urvashi after he goes to Swarga.

Once upon a time, Muni Raibhya, who was patient and a storehouse of tapa, did a tapa behind the Himalayas without eating anything and keeping all his sense organs under control. On observing the great penance of Raibhya Rishi, the lord of the Deva i.e., Indra felt frightened. He sent Urvashi to put obstacles and distract him from his tapasya. On being sent, that lady with an elephant like gait, started living at the excellent Ashram of the Raibhya Muni on the slopes of Himalayas. Creepers there were full of freshly sprouted leaves, birds chirped all around, the music produced by the Kinnaris is being taken in by the groups of antelopes who stand still to listen. The pollens of the flowers of Punnaga[17], Kesar[18] and Ashoka[19] together create an impression of the overgrown creepers in a garden. It appears as if Brahma has created another golden mountain.

Inaccessible to the common people, Urvashi shone in her own radiance like the one with the bow of flowers[20]. She was like the river of nectar flowing there. Adorned with the white pearls, her body carried a golden aura. She is full of tasteful youth as she wears her eternal youth.When she reversed her gaze to look back with a white lustre, her lips trembled like the freshly sprouted leaves of a creeper. Bunch of mangoes hung from both her ears, attracting the buzzing bees to both her ears eager, to take the nectar. She was like the creeper of Parijata[21] flower emerging out of womb of nectar. She had a narrow waist, broad hips and her breasts well rounded and white in complexion appearing as if they are the sharp arrows of the one with a bow of flowers i.e. Kamdev.

When Raibhya Rishi saw this large eyed Urvashi near his Ashram, he thought to himself that the three-eyed lord of love, who has once been burnt to ashes by Shiva, has once again created this beautiful lady. He saw her making the girdles and earring from the flowers and creepers in his garden. Looking at her the senses of the Muni got excited. This infuriated him and in the heat of anger he cursed her.

Raibhya said –You have come near me with an intent to put obstacles in my tapa. You who is full of pride for her beauty, may you instantly become ugly.

Agastya says – That auspicious looking woman, on being cursed thus in anger by the Muni, folded her hands together and spoke politely with respect.

Urvashi said –Bhagwan, please be pleased. I am a woman under someone else's total control. Please tell me how can I get rid of your curse?

Raibhya said –Ayodhya is a very auspicious and holy tirtha. Go and take bath there and you will regain your beauty. Water there will become famous by your name, it is imperative.

Agastya says –Then, respecting the words of the Brahmin, Urvashi proceeded to Ayodhya. She followed all the required rituals and she regained her lost beauty instantly. The place where she took bath came to be known as Urvashi Kund. Anyone who takes bath here gains, without a doubt gains immense beauty. On the third day of the bright half of Bhadrapada month is the annual pilgrimage day of this tirtha, when Vishnu should be worshipped for the fulfilment of all desires. Anyone who does so, gets to serve in the Vishnuloka. Weather it is a man or a woman, everyone attains here, what they desire.

Ghoshark Kund

Oh, lion among the Munis, to the south of Urvashi Kund, GhosharkKund is situated. They say it takes away all your sins forever. By taking bath and making donations here, one gets spoken about in the Suryaloka. There is no tirtha like this anywhere. Wounded, lepers, poor and those under the burdens of miseries – all of them, if they take bath here as per rituals, will have all their wishes fulfilled. On Sunday specially one should take bath here with reverence. On the sixth day of the bright half of the months of Bhadrapada and Magha, those who are desirous of finding a place in the Suryaloka should make an effort to take a ritual bath here. One should specially take bath on the Sundays of the month of Pausha. Taking a bath on the Sunday that falls on the seventh of any fortnight is extremely auspicious.

In the past, a king named Ghosh was born in the solar dynasty. Whole of earth, girdled by the sea, was under his rule. His fame shone through the spheres of the three worlds. His fame and influence were so bright that he appeared like another Sun. His mighty arms could break the groups of enemies. Once this ruler of the earth, left the administration of the kingdom to his ministers and headed to the thick forests full of trees all around, for hunting.

Due to the sins of the past life, the lotus hands of the king were infested with worms, an inauspicious sign for a king who was otherwise very handsome and free of ego. King was wandering around in the forest all by himself hunting boars, lions and deer. He felt extremely thirsty and weak in body and saw a lake close by.

Many sages were engaged in taking ritual bath in this lake and doing their daily Sandhya[2] pujas. The king performed the achmana[23] and took a ritual bath in the lake. He rejoiced as his body became divine and his mind felt delighted. He learnt from the sages that this is a Surya Tirtha and he started reciting a Stuti that would be dear to the Sun.

King said –

Namah to Bhagwan, the devata of the devas, to the consciousness

Namah to the Savitr[24], to Surya and to the one who gives joy to the world

Namah to the devta who divides[25], the one who resides in three Bhutas[26]

Namah to Vivasvan[27], the master of the yoga, one who lives in the form of Sat[28]

Namah to the best one[29], to the ultimate Ishwar, to the one who dispels darkness of three worlds

Namah to the brilliance of the Bhaskara[30], I praise the one beyond comprehension

Namah to the one who holds Yoga dear, who is Yoga and who knows Yoga

Namah to the Omkar, to the Vashatkar, to the one who is the form of knowledge

Namah to the Yagna, the Yajmana[31] of the Yagna, the Havish and the Ritvik[32] of the Yagna

Namah to the form that is destroyer of illness, to the one who gives joy to the lotus[33]

Namah to the one very gentle and very sharp, to the lord of the Suras

Namah to the receiver of the sacrifices[34], protector of the devotees, the dear Atman[35]

Namah to the one who lightens up the world for the welfare of the world

Be pleased with me. I bow down to you with all by devotion.

Agastya says –As he said so, the Sun was very pleased. He suddenly appeared there to do things dear to his devotee. He spoke these sweet words:

Sun said – Oh King, ask me for a boon. I am here because I am very pleased with you. Right now, I will give you the boon that you want.

King said –Bhagwan Bhaskar, the limitless, if you want to bless me with a boon, please stay here forever in my name in the form of a Murti.

Sun said – So be it, Oh King of the humanity. Your wish is very pleasing to the mind. Anyone who reads this Stotra composed by you, I will be pleased by their devotion and grant all their wishes. This place will be well renowned by your name on this earth. Anyone who takes bath here will have all his desires fulfilled.

Oh King, my devotees should take bath here and all that they wish for, they will attain everything.

Agastya says –After giving the boon with a lot of grace, the Bhaskara adorned with the thousands of rays, disappeared from there. Inspired by the body of Bhaskara, king created an excellent Murti and starting worshipping it. The place became famous as Ghoshark Kund in the world after the name of the king. Those who take bath here, get to serve in the Suryaloka. So, as per the established norms, devotees should worship this Murti of Sun with a pure mind and devotion. Whoever will take bath in this nectarine kund, will first gain untarnished fame and then will get to serve in the Suryaloka.

Reference

1. Yagna done with a desire to get a son
2. Agni or the Fire Deity
3. Offering, also Ksheer here
4. Dashratha had three wives, so one wife got 2 parts and two got one each
5. Also known as Kheer or rice and milk pudding
6. Brihaspati or Jupiter is the Guru of all the devatas
7. The yearly transition of planets in one's astrological chart
8. A commitment or citing a purpose for doing a particular ritual
9. Flax flower in deep blue color
10. Treasure
11. Most of the times interpreted as Nine Nidhis of Kubera consisting of various minerals extracted from earth.
12. Guptadana – a donation that you make quietly without putting your name on it
13. Listening – refers to listening to chanting of names or mantras
14. Wife of Vasishtha Muni
15. A form of Shiva
16. Special powers. Some of the Siddhis are – Anima (ability to make your body small), Mahima (to make your body bigger), Laghima (to make your body weightless), Garima (to become infinitely heavy or immovable), Prapti (ability to travel anywhere), Prakamya (ability to get all that one desires), Isitva (to have control over minds of others)
17. Calophyllum inophyllum or a variety of Champa
18. Saffron
19. Saraca Asoca
20. Kamdev – who is also called Kusumayudh or the one with bow of flowers
21. Night Jasmine
22. Sandhya refers to the transit time when the day turns into night and vice-versa. Most daily rituals are done at these times and called Sandhya
23. A purification rite performed by holding water in hand

24. One of the twelve Adityas
25. Refers to division of day and night created by Sun
26. Referred as three Bhutas – earth, a level above and below earth. Some also interpret it as three Vedas.
27. One of the 12 Adityas or forms of Sun
28. Truth
29. Para – can mean half Kalpa, Brahmana or the best
30. Another name of Sun
31. Host of the Yagna
32. The one who performs the Yagna
33. Refers to lotus opening with the rays of the Sun
34. Satras
35. Innermost essence or real self

Chapter 8

Kunds & Devi Spaces of Ayodhya

Rati & Kusumayudh Kund

Agastya says – Oh king among the Brahmins, to the west of Ghoshark Kund is situated the famous Rati Kund, known to take away all your sins. By taking bath here and making donations one gains bodily splendour.

To the west of that, there is a famous kund by the name Kusumayudh, the bestower of fulfilment of all desires, where taking a bath and making donation as per norms, one becomes beautiful just like Kandarp[1]. There is no doubt about that. Oh Brahmin, the ones who takes bath in both Rati Kund and Kusuma yudh Kund with devotion, definitely gains all the happiness. Couples who take bath in these Kunds together will become beautiful and famous like Rati and Kamdev. Those who are desirous of Dharma should take bath here and make donations with the purpose of pleasing Rati and Kandarp.

Couples thus taking bath will please Rati and Manmath[2]. A bath on the fifth day of the bright half of Magha month grants auspiciousness. Couples should first take bath in Rati Kund and afterwards in Kandarp Kund, very carefully. One should perform the worship of Rati and Kandarp with all the rituals. Clothes and embellishments should be offered to a Brahmin couple after worshipping them. By doing so, all the desires are fulfilled, there is no doubt in that. Brahmin couple should be worshipped with sandal paste, aguru[3], camphor, musk, vermilion etc, and different types of clothes and flowers. By doing so, there is no doubt that Rati and Kandarp would be satisfied, and Oh Brahmin, the couple will become comparable to Rati and Kandarp.

Mantreshwar

To the west of Kusumayudh Kund is the famous place called Mantreshwar, a place like which is difficult to find on earth. Anyone who takes bath here and does the darshana of Mantreshwar, will not need to take birth in hundred crore kalpas to come.

In the past, Ram known for his pure deeds, on completion of the work of devatas was in discussion[4] with Kaal[5] with regards to his return to heaven. The conqueror the senses, Ram then took a bath here and installed the linga named Mantreshwar. To the north of it, is a beautiful lake full of lotus and lily flowers. Taking a bath there and making donations get you different types of benefits.

On the fourteenth day of the bright half of Chaitra month is the day of annual pilgrimage here. Sacred bath and donations along with worship of Brahmins gets infinite benefits in the heaven, do not have any doubt about that. Oh Brahmin, no one is capable of describing the glory of this Mantreshwar tirtha that is bestower of the best merits. A linga like Mantreshwar has never existed in the past nor will happen in the future. This fulfiller of all desires should be worshipped with fragrance, flowers, incense and different pastes with all efforts. The one who worships so has the liberation on his palms.

Sheetala

To the north of Mantreshwaris the residence of Sheetala Devi. Wise men worship her to get rid of all the sins. She can be worshipped at any time but those who want to accomplish all that they wish should specially worship her on Mondays. Whenever there is a fear of an outbreak of an Epidemic (small pox), worshipping the Devi destroys the fear of the diseases.

Bandi Devi

To the north of Sheetala Devi resides Bandi Devi. Merely by remembering her, the fear of any kind of bondage goes away. Even those who are bound by chains due to the king being annoyed, they also get instantly released as soon as they remember Bandi Devi. That is why, one should make an effort to visit the Bandi Devi, especially on a Tuesday for the accomplishment of all desires. She should be carefully worshipped with fragrance, flowers, incense, lamps along with Naivaidya[6] of different kinds. Oh, the best among the Munis, for the affection of Bandi Devi, one should feed the Brahmins. By doing so, there is no doubt that all that you wish will be received by you.

Choodaki Devi

To the north of Bandi Devi resides the famous Choodaki Devi on this earth. It is said that merely by remembering her one can attain great Siddhis. Whenever there is a doubt in completion of a task or a fear thereof, merely by remembering Choodaki Devi, the work is achieved. One should stand in front of her and create sound by snapping the fingers and thumbs, and light the lamps. By lighting the lamps here all that is wished for is achieved. Her pilgrimage day is every fourteenth of every fortnight.

Maharatna Tirtha

To the east of Choodaki Tirtha is very famous Tirtha by the name Maharatna, which is considered best among the Tirthas. Taking bath, donating and worshipping the Brahmins here helps attain all your goals, there is no doubt about it.

On the fourteenth day of the dark half of Bhadrapada month is its annual pilgrimage festival. This annual festival is known as Maharatna festival and that is why this Tirtha is known as Maharatna. One should satisfy the Brahmins here by giving donations as per one's capabilities. Women should do the Jagran here with an aim to get valour, good fortune, prosperity all other types of happiness. Men should take bath here with all devotion.

Durbhar & Mahabhar Sarovar

To the south west of Maharatna is auspicious Durbhara lake and close to it is beautiful Mahabhar lake. By taking bath in these lakes, one definitely attains a place in the Swarga, so one should donate different types of things including clothes here. After taking bath in both the lakes, one should perform the Shiva Puja with different emotions and with utmost devotion. Maheshwar should be worshipped with fragrance and auspicious flowers. Neelkanth[7], the slayer of the Andhakasur is worshipped by the Yoginis. This way one should meditate upon Shiva along with his other half Parvati. One will not only have all desires fulfilled but also get to serve the Shivloka. By doing so, one can get rid of the sins accumulated. At the Mahabhar and the Durbhar Tirtha, on the fourteenth day of dark half of

Bhadrapada month, one should perform the worship of Shiva as well the Brahmins with all the devotion. One who does so, gets to live in the Shivloka, and is never disillusioned. Eternal Vishnu and Rudra are pleased forever with him. Merely by remembering them all the sins go away.

What more do I say, Oh Brahmin, this tirtha takes away all your sins and grants you all that you wish for?

Mahavidya Tirtha

Now I will tell you about another holy tirtha, where it is not possible to go on a pilgrimage or do donations, without having a good fortune. To the north east of Durbhar lake is eminent Mahavidya Tirtha. By the mere darshana of this tirtha, all the Siddhis accessible as if they are on your palms. In front of it is a lake, anyone who takes bath here and takes the darshanaof Mahavidya with respect and devotion, attains the ultimate goal.

Siddhapitha here is very famous too,it evokes respect and devotion. Here one should perform the worship as per the rituals with ultimate devotion. One can chant any mantra of Shiva, Shakti, Ganapati or Vishnu, as per one's own faith. By worshipping with full concentration of mind, one is bound to attain Siddhi, almost magically. So, one should perform japa here with complete focus. The monthly pilgrimage of this Siddhapitha happens on the eighth and ninth tithi. Different types of foods and fruits should be offered. Deity should be given a ritual bath with milk and then worshipped with devotion. One can attain Ucchatana[8] and Mohana[9] Siddhis here. Even chanting bad mantras can lead to Siddhi here. This is a very spiritual place to attain both the Moksha and the Siddhi of Vashikaran[10]. Japa, homa and donations done here give infinite merits.

Visiting this place during the Navaratri of the bright half of Ashwin month helps you get rid of all the sins.

Dugdheshwar Mahadev

In the past, after conquering the Ravana - the one who had made people cry, Raghupati returned here along with Sita and Lakshman. Bharat, along with his followers and adorned with Sri, came here on foot with an intention of meeting Ram. The divine cow Surabhi also came here and her udders were flowing with ample milk, making the milk fall on earth. Looking at milk falling on earth, vanaras and rakshasas were very surprised and they asked the lord of mobile and immobile worlds i.e. Sri Ram – Oh King, what is this?

Ram said that only Vasishtha Muni knows about it. Let us ask him. After this, with Ram in lead, they all approached Muni Vasishtha, and sat in front of him with folded hands. Vasishtha meditated for few moments and then calmly addressed Ram, who was leading the people with question in their mind.

Vasishtha said –Listen Oh mighty Ram, this is the auspicious Kamdhenu. She has come here for your affection, with her udders full of milk. Look in the middle of the milk, Rudra himself has come to see you. You have done the excellent work for the Devas by destroying the dynasty of enemies. Now in this pond you immediately worship the auspicious Shiva. In this holy pond of milk, he will be known as Dugdheshwar.

Agastya says–Then the Raghupati worshipped the linga named Dugdheshwar as per the directions of Muni Vasishtha. Sita too paid her respects to the kund, and that is why the kund came to be known as Sita Kund in the world. Anyone who takes bath in Sita Kund and takes the darshana of Dugdheshwar will get rid of all his sins, there are no two ways about it. Taking a bath, performing japa and homa, making donations here never go waste. By worshipping Sita, Ram and Lakshman here along with Dugdheshwar, all the desires in one's heart are fulfilled.

Its annual pilgrimage falls on fourteenth day of the month of Jyeshtha. Anyone who serves the Sita Kund as per the norms, he attains the ultimate goal, there is no need to think about it.

To the east of Sita Kund is tirtha of Sugriva called Sugriva Charita, where he resides. Anyone who takes bath here, makes donations and worships Sri Ram, all his desires will be fulfilled.

To the west of Sugriva Tirtha is Hanumat Kund, and to the west of Hanumat Kund is auspicious Vibhishana lake. By taking bath, making donations and performing the worship of Ram at both these tirthas, you accomplish all that you wish for.

This Ayodhya is like the Dharma Nidhi – the storehouse of Dharma or righteousness – remember that.

On listening to this sentence of Vasishtha Muni, Vibhishana and other followers of Ram, with all humility and respect asked him – Oh wealth of Tapa, please tell us this rare story. Tell us the glory of Ayodhya, tell us all about it, we are eager to hear it. Tell us how one should do the pilgrimage here and in what order it should be done. Please shower your grace on us and tell us all about it.

Vasishtha said –Listen all you Munis gathered here, the excellent glory of Ayodhya. Merely by listening to it, one gets rid of all the sins, there is no doubt about it. This excellent kshetra of Ayodhya is a mystery. It is the bestower of liberation for all living beings. Those desirous of Vishnuloka, like Sidhhas, they always take the vows of Vishnu and wear different adornments here. They practice yoga by controlling their breathing to subdue their senses. This place has different types of trees where all kinds of birds live. All the beautiful ponds here are full of blue lotuses. All the auspicious celestial damsels frequent them often. What more can be said about a place where the Hari himself lives eternally. Devotees of Vishnu offer all their actions to Vishnu here for the attainment of liberation, this is not possible elsewhere. This is the most excellent kshetra of Hari. This Ayodhya is a great Kshetra, an excellent place.

One does not get liberation as easily by taking bath at Naimisharanya, Kurukshetra, Gangadwar[11] or Pushkar. It is especially possible only here. At Prayag too, the liberation you get by doing various rituals is found here just by dedicating yourself to Hari. This Mahatirtha is way ahead of all other tirthas.

Munis with unmanifest bodies, Siddhas and Rishis, the way they achieve liberation here in Ayodhya, I do not think they can get it elsewhere. Those who serve Ayodhya with this goal, Sri Hari bestows them with best of yogic power and blesses them with his Sayujjaya Mukti, where the living being merges back with the Hari.

Brahma along with Devas, Rishis, Lakshmi, Vayu, Sun, Indra and other Devatas, they all come here to respectfully worship Hari. Sidhhas and Yogis living elsewhere too, focus their minds and worship this khsetra. Someone who has spent his life collecting sins, whose mind has been struck in the worldly matters, one has given up righteousness, he also will not return to this world if he spends his last days here. Those who follow Agamas[12], who follow Sattras, who work on winning over their senses, or those who take vows without following any of these, all of them attain the Hari here. This way the wise ones when they break out of their bodies, attain the liberation and reach the world of Hari. The liberation that Yogis may not achieve even after practicing for thousands of births can be achieved easily by just leaving the body here.

I have narrated the glory of this excellent and holy tirtha, that helps you attain the ultimate goal. I have not seen a place as holy as this one anywhere else. Those who want to earn merits they should patiently come here for pilgrimage and visit all the places in the prescribed order.

On the first day, one should observe Upvasa[13], take a bath and give donations as per one's capability. Upvasa means staying away from doing any bad deeds and giving up Bhoga or all the things that are enjoyed by the sensory organs. When one sits with all the good things in body and mind, it is called Upvasa. One observing the fast should take the ritual bath in Chakratirtha and donate as per one's capacity to give.

One should worship the Brahmins and do the darshana of Vishnu Hari. Then one should take bath in Swargdwara and again perform the worship of Vishnu with all efforts. At the Dharmahari tirtha, one should bodily cleanse oneself[14]. After this one should take bath in Papamochana, Rinmochana and Sahastradhara Tirthas and perform the worship of Anant Shesha. After this one should do the darshana of Chandrahari and Dharmahari. Then one should visit the Chakrahari and give donations as per one's capacity, one should take bath in Brahma Kund for the fulfilment of all desires. One should then perform the night long Jagran near Mahavidya. Next morning the Vrati[15] should get up and take a ritual bath in Swargdwara, and with all devotion perform the rituals for the ancestors and give donations accordingly and then perform the worship of Vishnu and Brahmins. One should worship the Brahmin couples and offer them clothes with complete devotion and ample dakshina should be given to them. After finishing all these rituals only one should sit down to have his own food.

Next day one should get up early morning and with full devotion visit the Rukmini Devi and other deities and different tirthas in order, taking bath and making donations as much as you can and worshipping Vishnu with a pure heart. With a clean mind, speech and body one should complete the pilgrimage. If one dies while on the pilgrimage, one is bound to attain liberation.

Agastya says – After listening to this Mahatmya from Vasishtha, the rakshasas led by Vibhishana and Vanaras led by Sugriva performed the pilgrimage as prescribed. They became pure with divine bodies and accrued merits that would ensure them a place in Swarga.

Reference

1. Another name of Kamdev or God of Love
2. Another name of Kamdev
3. A kind of fragrant Aloe Wood
4. Word used is Mantrana meaning consultation or discussion, the name of the Linga is derived from this word
5. Time or Lord of Time
6. Food that is offered to the deities, before offering it is Naivaidya, after offering it is Prasad.

7. Another name of Shiva meaning the one with blue throat
8. Eliminating the enemies
9. To control someone by creating illusion or delusion
10. Control someone else in body and thought
11. Haridwar is also known as Gangadwar i.e. where the Ganga enters the plains.
12. Ritual texts followed mostly by temples
13. Upvasa – usually referred to as fast
14. Kshorkarma refers to removing hair from the body, may be interpreted as shaving for men
15. Person observing the vrata or vows of pilgrimage

Chapter 9

Tirthas Around Nandigram

Gaya Koop

Agastya says –To the north east of Jatakund is the famous Gaya Koop, known to bestow the fruits of all desires. By taking bath in Gaya Koop and performing the rituals for one's ancestors here with one's senses under control, one can achieve anything that one desires. If any of your ancestors have landed in Naraka[1], they will go to Swarga, once their rituals are performed here. By performing the shraddh here, one is relieved of the debts of the ancestors. As per one's capacity the pind dana[2] should be performed. Sages direct that shraddh should be performed with barley, payasam made with milk and jaggery. By doing so, the ancestors are satisfied and pleased.

One should perform the shraddh with all faith and devotion. It satisfies not just the ancestors but also the devatas. When the ancestors are satisfied, they bestow prosperity and sons. Ancestors pleased with the shraddh beget you many sons, and one gets to enjoy the worldly pleasures amply. So, one should always make efforts to do the shraddh with all the rituals as prescribed. So, all those who are desirous of bounty of good deeds, should perform the shraddh with devotion. One performed at Gayakoop is especially beneficial for lasting results. On the Monday that falls on a new moon day, doing the shraddh brings infinite benefits. On the other Mondays as well, shraddh can be performed ritually, it satisfies the ancestors and you reap infinite benefits.

Pishachmochan Tirtha

To the east of Gaya Koop is the excellent and beneficial Pishachmochan Tirtha. Taking bath here and making donations ensures that one never enters the Pishacha[3] Yoni, so one should faithfully take bath here, give away donations and perform shraddh for ancestors with all devotion. Specially on the fourteenth day of the bright half of Margashirsh month, a bath here helps you stay clear of being a Pishacha.

Manas Tirtha

Close to it, in the east direction is the Manas Tirtha, it is the first among all the holy places, especially for taking bath. So, one should take bath here, and give donations for the fulfilment of all desires. Even if one has accumulated sins worth the size of Meru mountain, merely by taking bath here, one can get rid of all of them. All the sins gathered by way of speech, body or mind, whatever they may be, Manas tirtha can dissolve all of them. Holy and wise men perform the annual pilgrimage here on the full moon day of the Bhadrapada[4] month.

Tamasa River & Mandavya Muni Ashram

To the south of it lies the river named Tamasa, known as the destroyer of sins. Taking bath and making donations here, gets one rid of all the sins. Its banks are always beautiful and meritorious. Pious Munis from different places come here to live on its banks, and sacred ashram of Mandavya Muni is situated here. The banks of this river are enchanting with beautiful trees all around. The place where this river with beautiful waves originates is very pious and bestower of merits. Merely by looking at it, the sins dissolve away.

The place is adorned with bushes of all kinds, with different creepers hanging everywhere. There are Priyagnu[5] trees full of flowers and thorny Ketaki trees are in full bloom. Trees like fragrant Tamala, Karnikara, Bakula, Ashoka, Punnaga are in full bloom laden with flowers. Swarms of bees are hovering around them, eager to suck the honey out of flowers. Birds, embellished with the pollens of the lotus flowers are hovering on the fruits. Twittering of the birds like Saras[6], Mutkul etc. can be seen and heard all around. Somewhere the flocks of Brahminy ducks are circling, somewhere the geese are sitting on the Kadamba tree, somewhere the Karandaka ducks are making noise and somewhere buzz of the bees is filling the air. Bees move around intoxicated surrounded by the fragrance of the beautiful flowers. Somewhere rows of trees are adorned with creepers appearing like a Tilaka on the forehead. Different kinds of birds come here, the sounds of Harita pigeons fill up the forest. This sacred grove is thus enchanting to look at with all these elements. Somewhere the Neelkanth or Indian Roller birds are roaming in the bluish bamboo forests. Sitting on the branches of the flowering trees with fresh sprouts of fruits, they look beautiful. All this is splendid and enchanting in all directions. This is where Mandavya Muni did his tapasya, and the impact of that has made this place a holy tirtha.

To the east of this is the holy ashram of Gautam rishi, and to the east of that is the ashram of Chyawan rishi. Parashuram[7], your father, the treasurer of tapa, had first set up this ashram. On the banks of Tamasa river, there are different ashrams everywhere where ascetics perform their Tapa. This river called Tamasa is said to be very auspicious. The sacrificial pits excavated here add to its ambiance. So, by taking bath here, by making donations and by performing shraddh here, one accomplishes all goals, there is no need to think otherwise. On the full moon day of the bright half of Margashirsh month, a bath here is especially beneficial always. So, one should make an effort to take a bath here with a pure mind, and one will achieve all that one desires.

Sita Kund

Now I will tell you about another auspicious tirtha called Sita Kund, located near Dugdheshwar. On the fourteenth day of the bright half of Bhadrapada month is the annual pilgrimage day of this Tirtha. For the fulfilment of one's wishes and for removing all obstacles from your path, one should perform worship of the Vighneshwar here. Merely by remembering him, all obstacles go away.

Bhairav

To the south of it is a tirtha named Bhairav, who's mere darshana destroys all your sins, without a doubt. He is protected by the Vasudeva and he in turn respectfully protects his kshetra. So, one who makes all efforts to worship him with reverence as required, Bhairav bestows all the desires of his heart. Its annual pilgrimage happens on the eighth day of the dark half of Margashirsh month, that fulfils all kinds of desires. Bhairav should be worshipped with the food made from animals. This fulfils all desires, there is no doubt about that. One who stays in the temple of Bhiarav without any obstacles and worships him, gets everything he wishes for.

Bharat Kund & Jata Kund

To the north of this is the beautiful Bharat Kund. By taking bath here all your sins are destroyed, do not doubt that. Bath taken and donations made here give

Meeting of Bharat & Hanuman

eternal benefits. Here one should donate different types of food and clothes and offer cloths with adornments to the deity. In the past, Bharat - the descendant of Raghu, lived in Nandigram.Heart of this pure being who had control over all his senses was always focussed on Ram. Living here, he took care of all the subjects on earth. Bharat built this great kund that is now known by his name. He installed the Murti of Sri Ram and worshipped it with all his senses in control.

In this kund, all the great merits have come together to live. The pond is full of Lilies and lotuses in white, red and pink colors. Birds like geese, ducks and swans live here. The shade of the trees in the garden next to it add to its glory. One becomes pure and happy after taking bath in Bharat Kund. Anyone who takes bath here and performs the shraddh for ancestors not only satisfies the ancestors but also the devatas. Donations of different kinds of food and gold to Brahmins should be given with devotion.

To the west of it is the excellent JataKund, where Ram and others gave up their matted locks. JataKund is known to be the best among the Tirthas, and taking bath here and giving donations helps fulfil all desires. One should first take bath in Bharat Kund and worship Bharat, then one should worship Sita, Ram and Lakshman at Jatakund. The annual pilgrimage happens on the fourteenth day of the dark half of Chaitra month. So, with all prescribed rituals, one should worship Sita and Ram here, and then at Bharat Kund, one should worship Lakshman. After this couples should take a ritual bath in this nectarine pond that would enable them to live like an embodiment of good deeds in the Vishnuloka.

Reference

1. Equivalent of Hell
2. Rice balls
3. Flesh eating demons
4. Praushthpada is how Bhadrapada is referred here.
5. Beautyberry Trees
6. Stork Bird
7. Parashuram is the father of Ved Vyasa

Chapter 10

What is Real Tirtha?

Agastya says –Anyone who fasts without eating anything, or just taking the milk, while worshipping Ajita[1], the Siddhis are easily available to him on his palms. One should organize great festivals and sing accompanied by musical instruments. Any wise man who does so, all his wishes come true.

Mat Gajendra Tirtha

To the north of this (Bharat Kund and JataKund) is the auspicious tirtha of Mat Gajendra. There is a pond in front of it. One should take bath here with a stable mind and stay here for some time to attain complete Siddhi.After doing this one is never unhappy. This brave heart is the protector of Ayodhya and bestower of all desires. On the fifth day of the Navaratri is the annual pilgrimage of this tirtha. One desirous of accomplishing one's goals should worship here with fragrance, incense, flowers and naivaidya. Whatever one may desire, it is fulfilled here.

Sursa

To the south of this is the place of Rakshasi named Sursa, who is a great Vishnu devotee and a bestower of Siddhis. By worshipping her, men accomplish all that they wish for. The performer of best deeds, Ram brought her from Lanka and installed her here for the defence of Ayodhya. People observing the vows in Ayodhya, should go for her darshana and pray to her with due respect. For those desirous of wishes should conduct auspicious festivals for her, and make effort to do it with accompanying music and singing. On the third day of Navaratri is its annual pilgrimage day, which is the bestower of all kinds of happiness and progeny. So, one should perform this Utsava[2] with enthusiasm using different types of musical instruments and performing beautiful dances. By doing so, one is always protected.

Pindaraka

To the west of it is the place of brave warrior Pindaraka, who should be worshipped with fragrance, uncooked rice and flowers. By doing the worship of whom, all the Siddhis sit on your palms, he should be worshipped with all the due rituals. One should first take bath in Sarayu river and then worship Pindaraka, who deludes the ones engaged in sins and bestows wisdom to the one with good deeds. During the Navaratri, at the time of Pushya[3] Nakshatra, its annual pilgrimage is to be performed.

To the west of it, Vighnesh[4] is worshipped. Just his darshana is enough to remove all the obstacles. That is why worship the Vighneshwara to attain all desires.

In the north east direction of this is the place Ram took birth, called Janmsthan[5] which is the bestower of salvation. This birthplace is located to the east of Vighnesh, to the north of Vasishtha and to the west of Lomansh. After taking a darshana of this place, one does not have to enter womb again, even when one does not give any donations or perform any Tapa or go on any pilgrimage. On the Navami day, one should observe the fast and with the effect of baths taken and donations given one is liberated from the cycle of birth and death. Darshana of Janmbhumi[6] gives one the same benefits as donating thousands of Kapila cows every day. Merits that are accrued by doing Tapa in the Ashrams or by performing thousands of Rajsuya Yagnas and by Agnihotras performed every year are attained by mere darshana of the Janmsthan. The benefits that one gets by being devoted to parents and Gurus, the same is received by merely visiting the Janmbhumi.

Description of Sarayu

The darshana of Sarayu best ows merits of the satisfaction to the departed ancestors more than what they receive through a shraddh in Gaya, or the ones that are received by staying in Kashi for thousands of manvantars. The benefits that one gets by doing shraddh at Gaya or by darshana of Purushottam[7], in the Kaliyuga you get the same by just visiting the city of the son of Dashrath. The benefits that one gets by staying in Mathura for a Kalpa, the same can be obtained merely by the darshana of the Sarayu river. The benefits that one gets by spending the months of Magha and Kartik in Prayag and Pushkar, the equivalent merit can be earned by mere darshana of Sarayu. The benefits obtained by staying in Avanti[8] for thousands of crores of Kalpas is obtained just by witnessing the Sarayu. The merits that you earn by standing in the waters of Ganga for sixty thousand years can be received in half a moment in Kaliyuga, in this city of Dashrath's son.

Just by meditating on Ram for a moment, or even half a moment, one's ignorance is destroyed, which is the cause of this world. Here or there, no matter where you live, if one mentally remembers Ayodhya, one will not take birth again for hundreds of Kalpas. Sarayu is Brahman itself, giving liberation in the form of water. Effects of karma do not apply here and one who leaves body here becomes like Ram. Animals, birds, deer and those in lower species also attain divine liberation as per the words of Ram. After saying so that pot born Agastya Rishi paused.

Then, Krishna Dwaipaiyan said – Oh Taponidhi, this story that is inaccessible to listen for all living beings, I have heard it in proper way from the men who have visited it. Now I want to hear the order and the process of the pilgrimage in this Kshetra from you. Tell me the benefits and the order of the pilgrimage in detail. You are full of compassion, please be kind enough to tell me all this. Tell me in a way that after listening to you I can perform the pilgrimage in a proper manner, with your blessings.

Agastya says – Listen, I will tell you the order of pilgrimage of the seven Tirthas of Ayodhya. First of all, a pilgrim must be pure in mind, speech and body. His conscience should be free of any faults. With all sense organs under control, one should take cleansing bath in the Manas or Tirtha of mind. By following this, one attains the benefits of doing a Tirtha Yatra or pilgrimage.

Vyasa says –Tell me about the different mental or Manas Tirthas, by taking bath in which, one becomes clean in mind.

Agastya says – Oh sinless one, listen to the glory of the Manas Tirthas, by taking bath in which one attains the ultimate goal. These are:

Satya Tirtha or Truthfulness
Kshama Tirtha or Forgiveness
Indriya Nigraha or Restraint of Senses
Sarvabhuta Daya Tirtha or Compassion for all living beings
Satyavadita or Speaking the Truth
Gyan Tirtha or Knowledge
Tapa Tirtha or Austerity
These are the seven Manas Tirthas.
By being compassionate to all living beings, your mind becomes pure.

Merely a bath with water is not enough to purify our bodies. Only when the mind is pure, a ritual bath is meaningful. Now listen to the story of earthly Tirthas becoming meritorious.

Just like some parts of our body are good and others medium, there are places on this earth that are extremely meritorious. One who soaks oneself in both the physical Tirthas as well as Manas Tirthas, he attains the ultimate goal of liberation. Oh! Indra among the Brahmins, you too make an effort to go on this pilgrimage with pure heart and mind. I have not yet told the procedure for pilgrimage, now I will tell you about it in proper order.

Aquatic animals take birth in water and they die in water, even then they do not go to the heavens because their mind is not pure, it is full of impurities. Attachment to the worldly things is the impurity of mind. One who mnages to stay away from the worldly things can attain a pure heart. If the mind is cruel inside, no tirtha can purify it, just like a wine pot is considered unholy even if it is washed hundreds of times with water.

Charity, Yagna, Tapa, Cleanliness, Service at pilgrimage places, studying Vedas - all these are pious tirthas for the one who has a pure heart and mind.

One who has his senses under control, wherever he lives, that place is like Kurukshetra, Naimisharanya and Pushkar. Thus, I have told you the signs of Manas tirtha, by taking bath in which all the deeds performed by one are successful.

A wise person should get up early in the morning and take bath at the confluence[9], then take darshana of Vishnu Hari and then again take a dip in Brahma Kund. Take a bath at Chakra Tirtha and take the darshana of Chakrahari, followed by Dharmahari to get rid of all the sins.

Doing this pilgrimage on every Ekadashi or the eleventh of every fortnight is auspicious. A wise man after getting up in the morning, takes a dip in the waters of Swargdwara. After completing one's daily activities, one should go to see the city of Ayodhya. After visiting the Sarayu, one should visit the tirtha of Mat Gajendra. Then one should do the darshana of Bandi, Shitala and Batuk. After taking bath in the lake in front of it, one should visit Mahavidya, Pindaraka and Bhairav. Doing this on the eighth and fourteenth of the fortnight is beneficial.

On Angarak Chaturthi or the fourth Tithi that falls on a Tuesday, one should visit all the devatas mentioned above along with Vighnesh, to witness the fulfilment of all desires.

Wise one should get up early in the morning, take bath in Brahmakund, take the darshana of Hari and Vishnu Hari with pure mind, speech and body. He should then visit Mantreshwar, followed by Mahavidya. One who visits Ayodhya for the fulfilment of his wishes should visit Swargdwara and take bath here while wearing one's clothes and with senses under control. Different kinds of sins accumulated over different births perish when one takes bath here with one's clothes on. A pilgrimage thus performed removes all sins and bestows auspiciousness.

The one who performs this auspicious pilgrimage in prescribed way, he never gets to take birth even in hundred crore Kalpas. Hence, Oh Indra among the Brahmins, you too visit Ayodhya, without any further delay, perform the yatra in the right order with your senses under restraint.

Ayodhya is the ultimate place, Ayodhya is the most important place. A city like Ayodhya cannot be seen anywhere else. Ayodhya is the ultimate place as it sits on the Chakra of Vishnu. Oh Muni, thus I have described to you all that you asked for. Now, allow me to take your leave.

Suta says – After saying so, the pot born Agastya Muni became silent and Ved Vyasa spoke in a sweet voice.

Vyasa says – I am blessed, I am obliged and I am full of gratitude Muni. I understand now that truthfulness, cleanliness, studying Vedas, good behaviour, forgiveness, all this fail if one does not visit Ayodhya. I am pleased with what you have told about the dharma of this city. Now, I will visit this Ayodhya, free of all impurities. You too can proceed to your own Ashram now.

Suta says –This way, pot born Agastya Muni, after describing the right order and procedures of the great pilgrimage left for his ashram. Brahmin Vyasa proceeded to Ayodhya for attainment of all his desired goals. His eyes widened with surprise and pleasure upon reaching Ayodhya like a flower in full bloom. He performed the pilgrimage as prescribed. He was delighted to see the wonderful and great Tirtha. After completing the pilgrimage, he came back to his ashram and narrated the glory of Ayodhya in vivid details. I listened to the glory and proceeded to undertake the pilgrimage myself. Here at Kurukshetra, I have narrated the same for all of you.

Anyone who reads this unparalleled glory of Ayodhya or anyone who listens to it with all devotion, attains the ultimate liberation. So, one should make an effort to listen to it and perform the worship of Brahmins and Vishnu as prescribed. Gold etc should be donated to the Brahmins as per one's capacity to give. The one who wants sons will get sons, one who wishes for dharma will get dharma. Now, I have described in detail the glory of this land of dharma. Anyone who listens to this with great devotion, he gets all kinds of prosperity in life. He enjoys all the pleasures of life and in the end goes to Hari's abode.

The one who gives the narrator of this glory of Ayodhya, as per one's capacity to pay – money, vessels, beautiful clothes, silver, gold or cow, he too attains liberation.

Reference

1. Another name of Vishnu
2. Festival
3. One of the 27 Nakshatras or constellations in the sky
4. Ganesh
5. Literally means the birth place. In the context of Ayodhya it is Ram's birthplace.
6. Land of birth
7. Jagannath Puri
8. Another name for Ujjain
9. Of Sarayu and Gharghara rivers

Acknowledgements

It has to be a blessing, a true Ram Kripa to get an opportunity to write about the one of the oldest living cities in India, a city that is abode of Vishnu.

I would like to thank Dr. Y P Singh, Director, Ayodhya Shodh Sansthan for giving me this opportunity to translate Ayodhya Mahatmya in simple English. Dr. Singh and Ayodhya Shodh Sansthan have been instrumental is my exploration of Ayodhya. I could see most of the places, especially all the ponds, mentioned in the Skanda Puran. It was probably during this pilgrimage of mine that the seed for this translation must have been sown.

Thanks to my first readers Madhumita and Milind Tamhane. My husband Shashi not only read the manuscript but also supported me through the whole process of this project. Thank you, Kumar Amit for a thoughtful cover design and nit-picking my mistakes. Thank you Anupriya for the illustrations.

Thanks to Sampadananda Mishra ji for helping me with Sanskrit verses when I got struck. Thanks to everyone who is behind portals like 'wisdomlib', 'Spoken Sanskrit', 'Archive.org' and many other similar online resources. I have used their portals to understand words, phrases and for various references.

It has been a big learning journey. Translating meant I had to understand every word that was written with as little room left for interpretation as possible. This journey has not only brought me lot closer to Ayodhya but also to the way Indian Puranas are narrated from one generation to another. I hope I am passing that baton for this *Kaalkhand* or time period.

Jai Sri Ram!

Annexure

Tirtha wise Calendar of Ayodhya Yatra

Sl.	Place	Month	Paksha	Tithi	Remarks
1	ChakraTirtha	Kartik	Shukla	Dashami to Purnima	Kartik Mela for Snan& Dana
2	Brahmakund	Kartik	Shukla	Chaturdashi	Snan, gold and vastra dana
3	Rinmochana				Snan, gold and vastra dana
4	Paapmochana	Magha	Krishna	Chaturdashi	Snan, Dana
5	Sahastradhara	Shravan	Shukla	Panchami	Naga Puja
		Vaishakh			Snan, Donate Cow adorned with jewelry along with calf, worship a Brahmin couple for Lakshmi. All Tirthas come and live in Sahastradhara during the monthe of Vaishakh
6	Swargdwara				Early Morning (Pratah Kaal) Snan
7	Chandrahari	Jyeshth	Shukla	Purnima	ChandrasahastraVratUdayapan
8	Dharmahari	Ashadh	Shukla	Ekadashi	Snan in Swargdwara & Dharmahari Darshana
9	Swarnkhani or Gold Mine	Vaishakh	Shukla	Dwadashi	Snan, Dana
10	Sambhed Tirtha - Tilodaki Sangam	Bhadrapada	Krishna	Amavasya	Snan& Gold, Food donations
11	Sitakund	Margashirsh	Krishna	Chaturdashi	Snan, Dana, Japa, Homa
12	Guptahari	Kartik		Purnima	Snan, Cow donation
13	ChakraTirtha	Margashirsh	Shukla	Ekadashi	Snan, Dana
14	SarayuGhargha ra Sangam		Any month	Amavasya Purnima Dwadashi Ayana Vyapati Yoga	Snan
		Pausha		Purnima	Snan
		Pausha	Shukla	Trayodashi	Jagran, Snan, Dana
15	Goptratara	Kartik Jyeshtha	 Shukla	Purnima, Pavarni	Snan Jagran, Snan, Dana
16	Ksheerodaka	Ashwin	Shukla	Ekadashi	Snan, Dana

17	Brihaspati Kund	Bhadrapad	Shukla	Panchami	Snan, Dana
				Any Thursday	Snan, Dana, Puja for afflicted Guru in Gochar
18	Rukmini Kund	Kartik	Krishna	Navami	Snan, Dana, Homa
19	Dhan Yaksha	Magha	Krishna	Chaturdashi	Snan, Dana
20	VasishthaKund	Bhadrapada	Shukla	Panchami	Snan, Dana
21	Sagar Kund	Ashwin		Purnima	Snan, Dana
				Any Parvani days	Snan Dana
22	Yogini Kund	Ashwin	Shukla	Ashtami	Snan, Dana
23	Urvashi Kund	Bhadrapada	Shukla	Tritiya	Snan
24	GhosharkKund			All Sundays	Snan
		Bhadrapada	Shukla	Sashthi	Snan
		Magha	Shukla	Sashthi	Snan
		Pausha		Sundays	Snan
				Saptami that falls on a Sunday	
25	Rati – Kusumayudh	Magha	Shukla	Panchami	Snan, Dana, Brahmin Couple Worship
26	Mantreshwar	Chaitra	Shukla	Chaturdashi	Snan, Dana, Ling Puja
27	Sheetala Devi			Mondays	Worship
28	Bandi Devi			Tuesdays	Worship
29	Choodaki Devi			Chaturdashi	Chutki& Deep Dana
30	Maharatna Tirtha	Bhadrapada	Krishna	Chaturdashi	Snan, Dana, Jagran
30	DurbharMahabhar	Bhadrapada	Krishna	Chaturdashi	Snan, Dana, Shiv Puja
31	Mahavidya Tirtha	Ashwin	Shukla	Navaratri	Snan, Dana, Japa, Homa
				Ashtami, Navami	Offering food and fruits
32	Dugdheshwar Mahadev		Jyeshtha	Chaturdashi	Snan, Dana, Puja
33	Gaya Koop			Mondays & specially Mondays that fall on Amavasya or new moon day	Shraddh for ancestors
34	Pishachamochana Tirtha	Margashirsh	Shukla	Chturdashi	Snan
35	Manas Tirtha	Bhadrapada		Purnima	Snan, Dana
36	Tamasa	Margashirsh		Purnima	Snan, Dana
37	Sita Kund	Bhadrapada	Shukla	Chturdashi	Snan, Dana
38	Bhairav	Margashirsh	Krishna	Ashtami	Non-Veg Food offering
39	Bharat Kund				Snan, Dana, Clothes, Gold, Shraddh
40	JataKund	Chaitra	Krishna	Chaturdashi	Snan, Dana, Worship Ram, Lakshman, Sita and Bharat

41	Mat Gajendra	Navaratri		Panchami	Snan, Worship
42	Sursa	Navaratri		Tritiya	Festival with music and dance
43	Pindaraka	Navaratri		Pushya Nakshatra	Snan, Worship
44	Janmsthan			Navami	Darshana
45	Sarayu		•		Darshana

Month wise Calen dar of Ayodhya Yatra

Sl.	Month	Place	Paksha	Tithi	Remarks
1	Chaitra	Mantreshwara	Shukla	Chaturdashi	Snan, Dana, Ling Puja
		JataKund	Krishna	Chaturdashi	Snan, Dana, Worship Ram, Lakshman, Sita and Bharat
2	Vaishakh	Sahastradhara			Snan, Donate Cow adorned with jewelry along with calf, worship a Brahmin couple for Lakshmi. All Tirthas come and live in Sahastradhara during the monthe of Vaishakh
		Swarnkhani	Shukla	Dwadashi	Snan, Dana
3	Jyeshth	Chandrahari	Shukla	Purnima	Chandrasahastra Vrat Udayapan
		Goptratara	Shukla	Purnima, Pavarni	Jagran, Snan, Dana
		Dugdheshwar Mahadev	Jyeshth	Chaturdashi	Snan, Dana, Puja
4	Ashadh	Dharmahari	Shukla	Ekadashi	Snan in Swargdwara & Dharmahari Darshana
5	Shravan	Sahastradhara	Shukla	Panchami	Naga Puja
6	Bhadrapada	Sambhed Tirtha / Tilodaki Sangam	Krishna	Amavasya	Snan& Gold, Food donations
		Brihaspati Kund	Shukla	Panchami	Snan, Dana
		VasishthaKund	Shukla	Panchami	Snan, Dana
		Urvashi Kund	Shukla	Tritya	Snan
		GhosharkKund	Shukla	Sashthi	Snan
		Maharatna Tirtha	Krishna	Chaturdashi	Snan, Dana, Jagran
		DurbharMahabhar	Krishna	Chaturdashi	Snan, Dana, Shiv Puja
		Manas Tirtha		Purnima	Snan, Dana
		Sita Kund	Shukla	Chturdashi	Snan, Dana
7	Ashwin	Ksheerodaka	Shukla	Ekadashi	Snan, Dana
		Sagar Kund		Purnima	Snan, Dana
		Yogini Kund	Shukla	Ashtami	Snan, Dana
		Mahavidya Tirtha	Shukla	Navaratri	Snan, Dana, Japa, Homa
8	Kartik	ChakraTirtha	Shukla	Dashmi to Purnima	Kartik Mela for Snan & Dana
		Brahmakund	Shukla	Chaturdashi	Snan, gold and vastra dana
		Guptahari		Purnima	Snan, Cow donation
		Goptratara		Purnima	Snan

		Rukmini Kund	Krishna	Navami	Snan, Dana, Homa
9	Margashirsh	Sitakund	Krishna	Chaturdashi	Snan, Dana, Japa, Homa
		ChakraTirtha	Shukla	Ekadashi	Snan, Dana
		Pishachamochana Tirtha	Shukla	Chturdashi	Snan
		Tamasa		Purnima	Snan, Dana
		Bhairav	Krishna	Ashtami	Non-Veg Food offering
10	Pausha	Sarayu Gharghara Sangam		Purnima	Snan
		Sarayu Gharghara Sangam	Shukla	Trayodashi	Jagran, Snan, Dana
		GhosharkKund		Sundays	Snan
11	Magha	Paapmochana	Krishna	Chaturdashi	Snan, Dana
		Dhan Yaksha	Krishna	Chaturdashi	Snan, Dana
		GhosharkKund	Shukla	Sashthi	Snan
		Rati – Kusumayudh	Shukla	Panchami	Snan, Dana, Brahmin Couple Worship
12	Early Morning (Pratah Kaal) Snan	Swargdwara			Snan
13	Navaratri	Mat Gajendra		Panchami	Snan, Worship
		Sursa		Tritiya	Festival with music and dance
		Pindaraka		Pushya Nakshatra	Snan, Worship
		Janmsthan		Navami	Darshana
14	Any day	Sarayu			Darshana
		Bharat Kund			Snan, Dana, Clothes, Gold, Shraddh
15	All Sundays	GhosharkKund			Snan
16	Saptami that falls on a Sunday	GhosharkKund			
17	Mondays	Gaya Koop		Somvati Amavasya or Mondays that fall on Amavasya	Shraddh for ancestors
		Sheetala Devi			Worship
18	Tuesdays	Bandi Devi			Worship
19	Thursdays	Brihaspati Kund			Snan, Dana, Puja for afflicted Guru in Gochar
20	Chaturdashi	Choodaki Devi			Chutki & Deep Dana
21	Parvani days	Sagar Kund			Snan Dana
22	Any Month	SarayuGharghara Sangam		Amavasya Purnima Dwadashi Ayana Vyapati Yoga	Snan

Mapping of Indian and Julian Calendar

Sl.	Indian Month	Rough Julian Start Date
1	Chaitra	March 22nd
2	Vaishakh	April 21st
3	Jyeshth	May 22nd
4	Ashada	June 22nd
5	Shravana	July 23rd
6	Bhadrapada	August 23rd
7	Ashwin	September 23rd
8	Kartik	October 23rd
9	Margashirsh	November 22nd
10	Pausha	December 22nd
11	Magh	January 21st
12	Phalgun	February 20th

Days an Pakshas in Indian Calendar

Date	Indian Name
No Moon Day	Amawasya
1	Pratipada
2	Dwitiya
3	Tritiya
4	Chaturthi
5	Panchami
6	Sashthi
7	Saptami
8	Ashtami
9	Navami
10	Dashami
11	Ekadashi
12	Dwadashi
13	Tryodashi
14	Chaturdashi
15 / Full Moon Day	Purnima

Shukla Paksha – Bright Fortnight when Moon is waxing
Krishna Paksha– Dark Fortnight when Moon is waning
Navaratri – First nine days of Shukla Paksha of Chaitra and Ashwin months

Pilgrimage Order

In the chapter 8, Muni Vasishtha, tells Sri Ram and others about the sequence in which the Ayodhya Tirtha should be performed. The same is being listed here:

Chakratirtha

Vishnu Hari

Swargadwara

Dharma Hari

Paapmochana

Rinmochana

Sahastradhara

Chandra Hari

Dharma Hari

Brahma Kund

Mahavidya

Swargdwara

Rukmini Kund and other Tirthas

References

Complete Skanda Puran Vaishnav Khand, translated by S N Khandelwal, published by Chaukhamba Krishnadas Academy, Varanasi
Complete Skanda Puran Published by Motilal Banarasidass
Sankshipt Skanda Puran published by Gita Press
Other Versions available on Archive
http://spokensanskrit.org/
https://www.wisdomlib.org/
https://www.archive.org

Maps Details

Chakratirtha on Banks of Sarayu

To East of it – **Brahma Kund**

Rinmochana Tirtha - situated in the waters of Sarayu, seven hundred Dhanush north east of Brahma Kund.

Papamochana Tirtha - 200 Danush eastwards in the water of Sarayu

Sahastradhara Tirtha - To the east of Paapmochana Tirtha about 100 Dhanush away in the waters of Sarayu

Swargdwara- To the east of Sahastradhara, this Tirtha extends to 636 dhanush in the waters of Sarayu

Dharmahari- Towards the South East of this Chandrahari

Swarnakhani or Gold Mine - To the south of this Swargdwara

Sambhed Tirtha - south of Swarnkhani

Sita Kund - west of confluence of Tilodaki and Sarayu

Chakra Tirtha - To the west of Sitakund

Hari Smriti – West of Chakra Tirtha

Sarayu Gharghara Sangam - about three yojana to the west of Goptratara

Ksheerodaka - in the north-west direction from Sitakund

Brihaspati Kund - To the south-west of the Khseerodaka

Rukmini Kund– To South of Brihaspati Kund

Dhan Yaksha - the north-west of Rukmini Kund

VasishthaKund - To the North direction of Dhana Yaksha

Sagar Kund - to the west of VasishthaKund

Yogini Kund-To the south west of Sagar Kund

Urvashi Kund - To the east of Yogini Kund

GhosharkKund - To the south of Urvashi Kund

Rati Kund- to the west of GhosharkKund

KusumayudhKund - towest of Rati Kund

Mantreshwar - To the west of KusumayudhKund

Sheetala-To the north of Mantreshwar
Bandi Devi - To the north of Sheetaladevi
Choodaki Devi - To the north of Bandi Devi
Maharatna Tirtha - To the east of Choodaki Tirtha
Durbhar & Mahabar Sarovar - To the south west of Maharatna
Mahavidya Tirtha - north east of durbhar lake is eminent

Sugriva Charita - To the east of Sita Kund
Hanumat Kunda - west of Sugriva Tirtha
Vibhishana lake - west of HanumatKund

Gaya Koop – To the north east of Jatakund
Pishachmochan Tirtha - To the east of Gaya Koop
Manas Tirtha– East of Pishachmochan Tirtha
Tamasa River & Mandavya Muni Ashram - To the south of Manas Tirtha
Gautam Rishi Ashram - To the east of Mandavya Rishi Ashram
Chyawan Rishi Ashram - and to the east of Gautam ashram

SitaKund - located near Dugdheshwar
Bhairav - To the south of SitaKund
Bharat Kund - To the North of Bhairav
JataKund - West of Bharat Kund
Mat Gajendra - To the north of Bharat Kund and JataKund
Sursa - To the south of Mat Gajendra
Pindaraka - To the west of Sursa
Vighnesh - To the west of Pindaraka
Janmsthan – East of Vighnesh, to the north of Vasishtha and to the west of Lomansh

SARAYU
SARYU-GHARGHARA SANGAM
CHAKRAHARI
GUPTAHARI
BRAHMA KUND
RINMOCHANA TIRTHA
GOPRATAR GHAT/ CHAKRA TIRTHA
HARI SMRUTI
CHOODAKI DEVI
MAHARATNA TIRTHA
MAHAVIDYA TIRTHA
DURBHAR & MAHABAR SAROVAR
SAGAR KUND
BANDI DEVI
YOGINI KUND
URVASHI KUND
SHEETALA
MANTRESHWAR
KUSUMAYUDH KUND
RATI KUND
GHOSHARK KUND
MAT GAJENDRA
VIGHNESH
PINDARAKA
SURSA
TAMASA
GAYA KOOP
PISHACHMOCHAN TIRTHA
MANAS TIRTHA
JATA KUND
MANDAVYA MUNI ASHRAMA
GAUTAMA RISHI ASHRAMA
CHYAWANA RISHI ASHRAMA
BHARAT KUND
BHAIRAV